CONFESSIONS OF
A ROCK GUITARIST

CONFESSIONS *of a*
ROCK GUITARIST

STEVE LYNCH

Confessions of a Rock Guitarist

© 2025 by Steve Lynch

Library of Congress Control Number: 2025901810
ISBN: 978-1-964686-32-5 (paperback)   978-1-964686-33-2 (ebook)

This book is based on true events reflecting the author's memory of them. Some names and characteristics may have been changed, some events compressed, and some dialogue recreated.

Images used on the cover and in the book's interior are from the author's personal archive.

Editors: Robert Coconougher, Deborah Froese, David Remy
Cover and Interior Design: Emma Elzinga

Printed in the United States of America

First Edition

3 West Garden Street, Ste. 718
Pensacola, FL 32502
www.indigoriverpublishing.com

Ordering Information:

Quantity sales: Special discounts are available on quantity purchases by corporations, associations, and others. For details, contact the publisher at the address above.

Orders by US trade bookstores and wholesalers: Please contact the publisher at the address above.

With Indigo River Publishing, you can always expect great books, strong voices, and meaningful messages. Most importantly, you'll always find . . . *words worth reading.*

*This book is dedicated to my family, friends, and fans—
but especially to the one who stole my heart,
my love, Suzanne.*

Contents

Author's Note

Over the past several years, my family, friends, and fans have been encouraging me to write a book about the bizarre stories I've shared with them. I took their advice and began writing single-sentence reminders about my numerous experiences. The more I wrote, the more I remembered. Next thing I knew, I had over two hundred stories. I couldn't fit them all in one book, so I chose the ones I found to be most entertaining. The stories are laid out chronologically so you can follow them as they unfold.

Some confessions in this book have never been shared with anyone—until now. Musical experiences, personal growth, strange occurrences, humorous misadventures, mystical encounters, mysterious people, travels—through the good times and bad times, you will hear it all. This is the story of my curiously odd but humorous life. I invite you to join me on this journey. I think you'll enjoy the ride.

– Steve Lynch

Introduction

So here I am. January 18, 1984. It's my birthday, and I'm standing behind a massive stage with my Autograph bandmates, awaiting the green light to rush onstage and open the tour for the biggest band in the world: Van Halen. It's a sold-out crowd of 18,500 people in Jacksonville, Florida, and we've never played on stage together as a band.

As we stand at the base of the stairs leading up to the stage, we're trembling with both excitement and fear. We form a circle and put our hands together as if we were an army brigade preparing to conquer a formidable foe. On the count of three, we simultaneously yell, "Let's fucking rock!"

The lighting tech takes our cue and shuts down the auditorium house lights. Immediately, the crowd erupts into a thunderous roar that shakes the entire building as if a battalion of locomotives burst through its walls. In complete and utter darkness, the security personnel shine flashlights on the stairs and shout, "Go!"

We run up the stairs with an unprecedented burst of energy and get into position. The emcee bellows, "Ladies and Gentlemen, let me introduce to you . . . Autograph!"

With that, the stage lights come on, swirling and flashing chaotically, and bam! We explode into an outburst of thunderous drums, pounding bass, deafening chords, and screaming guitar riffs, leaving the audience in total awe.

I think, *so this is it. The Big Time!*

But how did I get here? What events in my life brought me to this moment? How did this become my reality? Well, to understand how it all happened, let's start from the beginning . . .

The Journey from Infancy to Delinquency

I can't remember a thing. Well, I do remember *some* things. And here is how it all began: I was born on January 18, 1955, in Williston, North Dakota. In addition to my parents, there were six of us kids. Now, if you think that's a large family, my paternal grandparents had eighteen kids. Guess there wasn't much else to do in the Badlands of North Dakota, other than be "bad."

At the age of one, I grew a bit bored with life in North Dakota, so I sat down with my parents to discuss the issue. I initiated the conversation by saying, "Let's move to Seattle. The World's Fair will open there in about six years, and I think it would be very exciting to attend on opening day."

Okay, we did move to Seattle when I was only a year old, but obviously, I never said any of this. I was still drooling and pooping myself—which I'm starting to do again. They say history does repeat itself. (Just kidding. Kinda.)

During my toddler years, it seemed as though I had some kind of a death wish, like a mini-Charles Bronson—except the vigilante in me was trying to off *myself.* On one occasion, while my mom was ironing,

I crawled up behind her and pulled the iron cord after she set it down. This brought the iron hurtling down toward me, causing the point to strike me just above my right eyebrow. There was so much blood Mom thought I was going to die.

Many years later, she told me that when this happened, I didn't cry. In fact, I didn't even make a sound. I guess I didn't feel it because it landed on my head. So, to set the record straight, the reason I am the way I am is not because Mom dropped me on my head when I was a baby. I took care of that myself, and still have the scar to prove it.

Another incident took place while Mom was cleaning dishes in the kitchen after breakfast. I crept out the front door and stealthily crawled behind Dad's car as he was warming it up. Once warm, he pulled out of the driveway and drove right over me. Mom was standing on the front porch, horrified by what she'd just witnessed! Dad, on the other hand, murmured, "Dammit!" but beyond that, was speechless: he had no idea how every tire managed to miss me. He seemed a bit disappointed by this.

Meanwhile, I was sitting in the driveway thinking, *What's everyone so freaked out about? I'm just chillin' here with my dirty diaper and pacifier.*

Then the '60s arrived. I was filled with awe and wonderment. In 1962, the World's Fair opened in Seattle, and we attended on opening day, just as I had planned in North Dakota when I was a year old (like that really happened). I thought it was the most amazing place on earth—complete with the Space Needle, the Monorail, the Pacific Science Center, carnival rides, and a massive dome-shaped water fountain for kids to play in. The fountain shot forceful projectiles of water right up your butt that would knock you over if you happened to be standing in the right spot. It was dubbed "The Children's Enema Fountain." Adults were there too. Some of them seemed to really enjoy the "water-up-the-butt" feature. They kept doing it over and over. I never quite understood this.

Everything was going great that day until I wandered off to buy cotton candy with no money and got separated from my parents. My parents were so upset they got the police involved in the search. They eventually found me in front of the cotton candy stand, where I was trying to coerce the vendor into *giving* me the cotton candy. My parents were not happy about this, and neither were the police. But in the end, I got my cotton candy—free of charge. At the age of seven, I'd figured out how to work the system.

To top off the day, we went to check out the last section of the fair and visited the Pacific Science Center. Inside, we watched a 3D film screening about an African tribe who'd become infected with elephantiasis, a disease that makes your legs swell up to look like those of an elephant. This freaked me out! For weeks, I had nightmares about contracting this horrific disease and would never be able to play soccer or ride my bike again. Of course, I never caught it. I suppose there was a tad too much real estate between Seattle and Africa.

The following year, Elvis Presley came here to film *It Happened at The World's Fair*. My mom, being a huge Elvis fan, had to go see him. But I didn't really care about him. My priorities were cotton candy and carnival rides, not Elvis, elephantiasis, or the colon fountain.

During this time, we lived at Green Lake, an area just north of downtown Seattle and the World's Fair. Right before moving there, my dad had been bouncing from one job to the next. We were in dire straits and on the brink of becoming homeless. After living in government housing, staying with relatives, and even living in our car briefly, we were rescued by Uncle Leonard, my dad's brother. He arranged for us to live in a house located next to Blanchet High, a Catholic school where he did administration work.

It's important to note that, later in life, I came to realize the hardships Dad went through to keep us fed and a roof over our heads. He worked three jobs at a time to provide for us. He never complained; he just did what needed to be done, no matter how physically or mentally taxing it was. He was our hero. Mom was also our hero. With six kids to care for, she was constantly cleaning the house, doing laundry, getting us off to school, making our meals, and spanking me, which was necessary because I was always doing stupid shit.

At this time, my childhood was both exciting and adventurous. I rode my bike down to Green Lake and pedaled around the three-mile circumference each and every day, rain or shine (which in Seattle was mostly rain). My friends and I then rode up to Woodland Park Zoo to visit Bobo and Fefe, the inseparable gorilla couple who were the main attraction.

On the walk to school each day, me and my friends stopped at the local hobby shop and asked the owner if he'd received anything new that morning. My main interest was model cars. Classic, new models, or hot rods—it didn't matter, I just loved building them. I saved my lunch money to buy the new models that arrived, even if it meant going hungry.

Riding our bikes around Green Lake, visiting Bobo and Fefe at Woodland Park Zoo, going to school at historic Daniel Bagley Elementary, and stopping by the hobby shop each day created some very pleasant childhood memories. Life was good. To this day, it still warms my heart and makes me smile when I reflect on those innocent times.

❧

One day, while living next to the Catholic school Blanchet High, I experienced a very disturbing encounter. As I was walking through the school to visit my uncle, a nun caught me in the hall and aggressively demanded an explanation as to why I was there. When I told her that I was simply going to visit my Uncle Leonard, whose office was at the end of the hall, she grabbed my shoulder and squeezed so tight I thought she was going to snap my collarbone. She then shoved me into a large room, which turned out to be the school church.

"You are trespassing in the House of God. Therefore, you are a sinner," she angrily scolded. "You must pray for your salvation and redeem yourself in the name of the Lord."

I thought, *For what? What the hell? Where did that come from? What a bitch!*

While I was in this *supposed* "House of God," I felt an eerie presence that scared me out of my wits. The place had a dark, ominous energy which I have never experienced before. I remember thinking, *Why am*

I so frightened? Isn't Jesus supposed to be here? The Light, The Lamb, the Son of God? I should be surrounded by positive energy and white light.

But there was no such presence. Instead, it was dark and foreboding. And why was I being put through this torment when I'd done nothing wrong? My understanding was that nuns were servants of God. I had two aunts who were nuns, and they were nothing like this woman. It just didn't make sense. The experience left me with a very bad impression—not of God, but of religion.

I told Dad about the incident and pleaded with him to let me stay away from anything involving the Catholic religion. Instead, we continued going to church every Sunday morning. All six of us kids had to get up early and take baths using the same bathwater, starting with the oldest first and on down the line (I'm glad I wasn't the youngest). Then, we dressed up nice and fancy and drove to church. All the while I'd complain about everything from evil nuns to getting up early when it's not a school day and swimming in dirty bathwater to missing Sunday cartoons and not understanding anything said in church because it was all in Latin.

"What was the point? I mean, *really*?" I asked.

One Sunday, while I was ranting as usual in the back of the car, Dad did something completely unexpected. He pulled our 1955 Ford Victoria to the side of the road and turned around to face me. I thought for sure he was going to smack me upside the head. But instead, he looked directly at me while pointing his finger.

"You are right," he said. "We don't understand a thing they're saying, so what *is* the point? Let's go to Arctic Circle and get ice cream instead."

We were ecstatic! Arctic Circle was the ultimate euphoria to a kid's taste buds.

From that day forward, we never went back to church. We did however go back to the Church of Arctic Circle every Sunday. And we no longer had to get up before dawn, swim in each other's filth, and listen to old men in white robes speak gibberish. My brother and sisters thought

I was the shit! As it turned out, we perfectly understood the language at Arctic Circle, and there was no reason to get up early to take a bath because the Church of Arctic Circle was always open, so they didn't care what time you showed up or what you smelled like. It was heaven.

During the early '60s, a tragic incident occurred that caused a sudden darkness to shroud our nation. It happened on November 22, 1963, while sitting in class at my elementary school. The principal walked into the classroom and whispered something in our teacher's ear. The teacher was so distraught by what was said she broke down uncontrollably. Naturally, the class was confused as to what was taking place.

The principal then turned to us and asked which student was responsible for the audio-visual equipment. Since this was my job, I raised my hand. After I rolled the TV into the room and adjusted the rabbit-ear antennae, I dialed in reception to the local news. What we watched over the remainder of the day was horrific. President Kennedy had been assassinated. There wasn't one person in that classroom or the entire school who wasn't deeply affected, and we all cried.

Everything had changed. Innocence was lost. Camelot was gone forever.

To say the '60s were an incredibly turbulent time in our history would be an understatement. There was the Bay of Pigs, the Cuban Missile Crisis, the assassination of JFK, the Vietnam War, flower power, free love, psychedelics, student protests, the Women's Liberation Movement, birth control, the Cold War, the Beatles, the British Invasion, the Haight-Ashbury hippie movement, Allen Ginsberg and the Beat Movement, Andy Warhol and Pop Culture, the assassination of Martin Luther King and Robert F. Kennedy, the Charles Manson killings, the space race and the moon landing, Woodstock, Stanley Kubrick's *2001: A Space Odyssey*, and the rise of Eastern philosophies, et cetera et cetera.

And where was I during all of this?

I discovered Jimi Hendrix and LSD.

I became enthralled with Hendrix the first time I heard "Purple

Haze" on the radio and rushed out to get his debut album, *Are You Experienced*. I couldn't wait to get home from school each day to play it repeatedly until I fell asleep. There was something about his style that I found mesmerizing. His selection of notes and the way he delivered them intoxicated me. I would close my eyes and let his playing take me into a dream world.

This experience changed my perspective of music, and it changed me.

Soon after my exposure to Hendrix, I became aware of other guitarists, like David Gilmore of Pink Floyd, Jimmy Page of Led Zepplin, and, last but not least, Jeff Beck of The Yardbirds and the Jeff Beck Group. It was not only their playing that inspired me, but their unprecedented and remarkably brilliant writing. It was magical. I didn't just listen to the music, I absorbed it. It elevated my consciousness and awoke something within me—and that *something* is still with me today.

↘

Around this time, my family moved to Alderwood Manor, an undeveloped area surrounded by wilderness north of Seattle. I was heartbroken to leave the Seattle area I loved so much but, after some adjustment, I realized how much I enjoyed living next to seemingly endless forests. The move played an instrumental role in my love for nature. Johnny, my younger brother, and I built numerous tree camps, blazed trails through the woods, and met new friends. One of them was a kid my age named Jerry.

Jerry and I ended up being musical *compadres*. We loved the Beatles and all the British bands that were popular at the time. We were bound and determined to write songs of that genre and become fabulously successful—which is many a kid's dream, then and now. Jerry already owned a guitar, so he thought it best if I got a bass guitar. That's how I got started playing bass in 1967, even though my true passion was guitar.

It was during this time that my friend Jerry and I constructed a tree house so we'd have a place to practice and play records. It had a living room, a kitchen, a bedroom with two cots, and running water and electricity. We also installed a rope swing that would carry us from the deck of the tree house through a ravine to the opposite hillside and back to the deck. But the slippery rope of the swing made it almost impossible to hold on. So, we tied a loop at the end to put a foot in to avoid slipping and falling into the abyss nearly two hundred feet below.

Shortly thereafter, my dad got another job offer that forced us to move yet again. This time, we relocated about a half-hour further north to a town called Marysville. My best friend and I would be separated, but we arranged it so we could spend weekends together playing and listening to music. I would spend one with him and his family, and he would spend the next with us. Everything seemed to be going quite well . . . until one day, when everything changed dramatically.

↯

While visiting Jerry one weekend, we decided to take his portable reel-to-reel tape recorder and play a little joke on his parents. After purposely eating a whole can of beans each, we proceeded to record the obnoxious flatulence that resulted. Later that night, we sneaked into his parent's bedroom while they were sleeping and placed the recorder under their bed. Then Jerry hit the play button and we scurried out as quickly as possible.

Complete pandemonium ensued. Through the crack of their bedroom door, we saw that the noise had awoken them, and they were blaming each other for the abhorrent farting. Jerry and I laughed so hard that tears streamed down our faces. We had such a hard time catching our breath that our faces turned blue!

Unfortunately, things took a turn for the worse. Jerry's parents were extremists when it came to their religious beliefs and were not entertained by our innocent little prank. They immediately took away Jerry's tape recorder, his records, his guitar, and his amp. Then they told him he would never play music again, and that our friendship was over.

We were devastated! We only meant it as a harmless joke. But having fun and being happy didn't quite fit in with their ridiculously strict principles.

The following week, things took a far more drastic turn. As I returned home from school one day, Dad told me he needed to have a talk with me. I could tell it was going to be a serious discussion by the look on his face.

As we sat on the sofa, he proceeded to tell me something I never expected nor wanted to hear: "Son, I have some bad news. Your friend Jerry has died in a tragic accident."

My world fell apart. I fell to the floor in a crumpled mess. He was my best friend. We were supposed to be the next Beatles. Nothing made sense.

Dad then informed me that Jerry had died from "accidentally" hanging himself from the loop we had tied in the rope swing for our feet. Guilt swept over me. It had been my idea to tie that loop. The detectives told Dad that Jerry's foot slipped out while he was swinging, and it caught his neck in the fall. They said it wasn't anyone's fault, that it was just a tragic accident. But it didn't ease my guilt.

Jerry's death would haunt me for decades. How could his foot slip out of the loop and just happen to catch his neck at the perfect angle? The odds of this were astronomical! What we had tied was just large enough to hold a single foot. So, how could it catch his neck while he was falling? I ran the scenario over and over in my head for years but could never make sense of it.

One day, I came to realize I couldn't make sense of it because that's NOT what happened. Jerry took his own life. Everything he lived for had been taken away from him—his music and his dreams. I think my dad and the police told me it was accidental because they thought a kid my age wouldn't understand suicide. But I understand it now. And I believe I've finally put the pieces of this complex puzzle together. In fact, I have no doubts whatsoever.

The experience made me realize there are times you may find answers and times you may not. Sometimes, you may find more questions than answers, and sometimes, you may figure it all out on your own. I believe I did just that. Jerry's suicide marked the first time in my life I'd ever felt desolate. I had an emptiness that could never be replenished. I withdrew from the life I had once known, never to be quite the same again.

2

From Here to Infirmary

In the Age of Aquarius, beatniks poured into the coffee houses of Greenwich Village (New York City) while flower children blossomed in Haight-Ashbury (San Francisco). What seemed harmonious was later deemed to be chaotic. Although there was coffee permeating the air to the east and marijuana filling the ether to the west, there was an undeniable stench in the atmosphere that spanned from coast to coast. The Vietnam War.

Throughout the '60s, I witnessed the pandemonium ensuring from the draft and the upheaval that followed. I watched footage of the war nightly with Walter Cronkite, Dan Rather, and Huntley-Brinkley. It was not pretty. Nor was it necessary, as I later found out.

What was I doing while all this havoc occurred? I was creating my own version of mayhem.

It all started when I met some new friends in Marysville. They weren't really friends per se. More like acquaintances. Or, more simply put, a gang of juvenile thugs with whom I regrettably got involved. I didn't like these people. In fact, I despised them. But at that point, I felt it safer to associate with those I didn't care much about. That way, if something tragic happened, it wouldn't affect me the way Jerry's death had. I'd become detached, reckless, and careless, and it resulted in some very reckless behavior.

The leader of this little gang was a bit older than me and as ruthless as they came. We called him "Chief" because he always had to be in charge. As a Native American from the Tulalip Reservation, he thought the title fitting.

The reservation was located across the railroad tracks from where we lived. Most referred to it as the wrong side of the tracks. But as I saw it, both sides were on the wrong side. In 1967, the little town of Marysville's main industry was logging, and being such, its existence was very bleak. There most certainly wasn't a Ward or June Cleaver anywhere to be found, and the kids at my school were a far cry from Wally and Beaver. Even Eddie Haskell would have been considered a saint in this godforsaken place.

My first involvement in crime with this so-called puberty-rising gang involved stealing lawnmowers. Now, you may be thinking, *Why lawnmowers?* The reasoning behind this is we wanted to use the engines to mobilize our go-carts, which worked fabulously! We rode them through the streets day and night like a mini Indy 500. We soon outgrew this adolescent phase and moved on to bigger things. Our glorious leader, Chief, decided we should take it up a notch by breaking into houses. I didn't like this idea at all; it went against my principles entirely, but he was the boss, so I reluctantly agreed.

For our first job, we broke into a nearby house late at night. Because I was the smallest and could easily squeeze through the window, I was chosen to go first. Lucky me. As I was trying to jimmy the window open, the front door violently swung open and this burly monstrosity with the stature of the Incredible Hulk stormed out onto the porch. He glared directly at me with the eyes of a pissed-off bull and belted out, "What the FUCK do you think you're doing!?"

It took me a split second to notice the shotgun in his hands before I dropped a turd and bolted.

The next thing I remember was hearing the gun go off and the vicious sting of rock salt penetrating my lower back and ass. I know for a fact I'd never howled so loud in my life. The gang and I ran down the street, screaming in unison—but why were *they* screaming? I'm the one who got shot!

We never went near that house or even dared walk down that street again for fear of the Hulk's mighty wrath.

Our dirty deeds resulted in a total of thirty-eight home break-ins, all of which produced marginal gains. We only absconded with a little cash or jewelry, all of which was returned once we were caught. We didn't even spend any of the money, except for a few dollars on candy. Although what we'd taken was considered petty, the experience left me with a tremendous sense of guilt. This wasn't who I was, and I knew better.

When we finally got busted, I found out the judge who was assigned to our case owned the last house we broke into. Shit! This was especially bad because our tribal leader, Chief, had gotten drunk that night and decided to go on a vandalism spree . . . in the judge's house! This did not play in our favor. I had to spend two weeks in a juvenile correctional facility. After that, I was supposed to be sent to the Juvenile Diagnostic and Treatment Center in Fort Worden for a year. The institution had a nasty reputation for harboring the worst of the worst inmates as well as the meanest guards. Luckily, I didn't have to join this fine fraternity. I was released after two weeks because it was my first offense. I was very thankful I wouldn't be spending a year in a cell with a creature named Bubba.

The time behind bars made me reflect on my bad decisions and realize this was not the path I wanted to travel. I decided to end my life of crime. It had only lasted six months, but I'd had enough. My philosophy is this: It's best to make mistakes when you're young. That way, you learn from them to make better choices in the future.

And perhaps you'll avoid sharing a cage with "Bubba the Buick" later in life.

At this point in my story, it was 1968, and I was now thirteen. This next part of my life was really a trip, as in an *acid* trip. I didn't have many alternate dimension excursions, but what I experienced was more than enough. Again, I'm not the way I am from Mom dropping me on my head when I was a baby . . . well, you know the rest.

I had a variety of adventures and misadventures with psychedelics, but I was not alone. Everyone seemed to be taking the psychedelic plunge. I even lost my virginity on acid, which was a strangely euphoric experience. It was with a girl I'd only run into occasionally at parties. On this exceptionally unusual night though, we became a bit more interconnected, in a manner of speaking.

While sharing the otherworldly mind-bending experience together, we decided to lie on her bed for a while to collect ourselves. After chatting for a bit, one thing sort of led to the next, and voilà! We became entangled in a uniquely blissful psychedelic interlude. It felt as if I was experiencing my first sexual encounter in a Salvadore Dalí painting.

Afterward, while lying beside her, I began to discuss how intense the experience was, but she didn't respond. I glanced over and noticed she was lying on her back just staring at the ceiling. I kept repeating her name and asking if she was okay, but I got no response. Then I started to freak out. I thought I had killed her—with my penis! *Murder by penis* is what I'd be charged with! I couldn't believe it. I was going to prison because of my penis, and I'd never used it before!

Then something completely unexpected happened. She moved a little, which made me fly right out of bed. Then I leaned over and nervously shook her gently. She turned her head in my direction with her eyes glaring. "What?" she asked.

I jumped back again. I was so high I thought she was dead but still communicating with me. Thankfully, she was alive. So, I proceeded to tell her she was staring at the ceiling with her eyes open and wasn't responding to me. She chuckled. "Oh, I sometimes sleep with my eyes open. I must've dozed off."

So, that's how I lost my virginity. I was at a party ripped on acid having sex in a Salvadore Dalí painting with a girl three years older than me who slept with her eyes open. I can't say I would recommend this method to anyone on a first date or anyone seeking to lose their virginity. Or anyone . . . for any reason at all.

Another one of the early trips I experienced took place at a friend's house party where everyone present had dropped acid. I remember when that little orange pill started to kick in—Orange Sunshine, it was called—and it wasn't a pleasant feeling. As I sat in the living room, I began to experience some freakishly vivid hallucinations. Everyone's faces started scabbing over, with puss and blood oozing from the scabs. I was so horrified that I immediately ran upstairs and locked myself in the bathroom. I began to sense an uncomfortable feeling in my mid-body. Just as I was growing concerned, I realized I had to pee. Duh! So, I lifted the toilet seat and proceeded to take care of business. Halfway through, the propped-up lid grew eyeballs. The eyeballs fixated on me. *Oh, Lord help me!* To make things worse, for no apparent reason, the toilet seat slammed down with such force it sounded like a cannon going off—the effect obviously exaggerated by the drug. This scared me so badly that the rest of my urination session landed nowhere near the toilet; in fact, it was anywhere but. Like a firehose without a fireman.

The seat then began to take on some new characteristics of its own. It rose up and down from the toilet as if it were a mouth trying to form words. Being in an oblivious state, I leaned in closer to try to understand what it was saying. It muttered in a haunting whisper, "Don't look in the mirror . . . don't look in the mirror . . ."

So, what did I do?

I looked in the mirror.

Bad idea. I saw my face melting, my eyes falling out of their sockets, and my scalp starting to reveal bone. I ran downstairs and out of that house so fast it seemed as if I was transported to the front yard instantaneously—no doors, no stairs, no people. I just appeared there. I sat in the front yard for quite some time, waiting for the hallucinations to subside, all the while desperately clinging to my sanity or whatever was left of it.

My friend Jimmy eventually came out of the house with a couple of other friends and noticed me sitting there, staring out into the cosmos. They sat next to me and discussed how powerful the LSD was and what everyone inside was experiencing, which, for most, wasn't exactly a weekend at Willy Wonka's.

After our little chat, we walked up the hill to where construction was underway for the new I-405 freeway. Once we reached the site, to our surprise, lo and behold, what did we find? A steamroller. We hopped aboard and noticed the key was still in the ignition, so we turned it and pressed the start button. Much to our delight, the diesel engine came to life with a plume of black smoke and a roar like a dragon awakened from its slumber. We thought it was the coolest thing ever. For the next couple of hours, we took turns navigating this lovely monster across the freshly laid blacktop. We then looked for things we could press into the soft pavement and found an old doll someone had discarded, which we immediately submerged into the asphalt. I can only imagine what the construction workers must have thought when they showed up the next day.

WTF?

After I'd come down to a state of semi-normalcy, I began my trek home. When I arrived, I slowly opened the front door so as not to make any noise and quietly closed it behind me. Then, out of nowhere, *wham!* Dad's hand smacked me so forcefully that I went straight to the floor, where I hit my head again with a thud.

"Don't you EVER come home this time of night again!" he said angrily.

As I lay there in la-la land with a multitude of stars revolving around my head, I thought, *Wow. You really do see stars if you're hit in the noggin' hard enough.* I don't know how long I lay there gazing at the orbiting celestial bodies, but it seemed like an eternity. And even though my head was pounding, I thought it was a beautiful site to behold.

The most electrifying experience I had while experimenting with psychedelics was on LSD-25, the purest form of acid. It took place on a beautiful sunny day when my friend Dave and I headed into the deep woods. There, we would be completely isolated while searching for the Holy Grail of altered states. Or, to put it simply, we went on a "nature trip." We each ingested a full cube of LSD-25 and awaited the forthcoming adventure. Obviously, we weren't exactly entering the Church of Latter Day Saints—or LDS; we were slithering into the Church of LSD.

As we sat among the trees, we started to home in on the wildlife sounds surrounding us. It was intoxicating. We got into a deep discussion about the euphoric feeling we were each experiencing, not only mentally but physically and spiritually as well. A short time later, we both wandered off in different directions, all the while absorbing everything this magical kingdom had to offer. I no longer felt separate from my natural surroundings; I was part of it. Every faction of life on earth seemed to make perfect sense, and it all fit together masterfully. Nature was a symphony of creations playing together in perfect harmony.

As I wandered about, I went up to an old maple tree and held one of its leaves next to my hand. While intently observing the leaf, I saw the chlorophyll flowing through its veins, and when I looked at my hand, I could see the blood flowing through my veins. At that very moment, I realized the leaf and my hand were one and the same. Blood and chlorophyll worked off the same principle, pulsating life into existence.

I walked up to an old Douglas fir and placed my hands on it, closing my eyes as I touched it. I could literally *feel* the energy from it connect with my own. Wow! What an incredible feeling! I was beyond elated!

My experience seemed to be that of a grand awakening, an

introduction to a deeper meaning, of truth and understanding. The drug caused neurotransmitters to connect to other parts of my brain that usually don't communicate with one another. As a result, reality felt more defined. I later realized the experience had given me a different perspective on how I viewed life, listened to music, and my approach to guitar. I became more open and more aware. Music and nature had now become an integral part of who I was, and what I would continue to become. And the emotional baggage I carried from the death of my friend Jerry seemed to fade away. I now understood the cycle of life.

And that's where my spiritual journey began.

I was only thirteen when all this took place, but it opened my mind to alternative thought and changed me in ways I never could've imagined. After that trip, I never took LSD again. I had no use for it. I'd gained all the insight I needed. My Norman Rockwell view of life had transformed into an abstract Picasso, and it all made sense.

❧

Entering the year 1969, I was fourteen years old, and my family was on the move. Again. My dad received another job offer to work for Union Pacific Railroad. So, the family packed up and moved to Des Moines, a little coastal town south of Seattle. When I started my eighth-grade school year, my hair was halfway down my back, which was way too long for school regulations. After I enrolled, they demanded I cut it off, but I refused. This refusal soon found its way to the district courthouse. I argued that the last school I attended allowed guys to have long hair and that it was our "right of expression."

All the other students were in support of me, but my dad was not happy with my shenanigans. Brandishing a pair of scissors, he sat on top of me, pinned my arms with his knees, and proceeded to cut my hair off. But I put up one hell of a struggle and got away with most of my hair still intact. I never held incidents like these against my dad, as he was only doing what he thought was right. And besides, I really was a little shit! (I know this because I still am.)

After a couple weeks of deliberation, the court ruled in my favor: long hair for guys was now accepted—not only for the junior high school I was attending, but for the entire school district!

All the students loved me, but the principal, vice-principal, and the entire teaching staff loathed me. Especially the phys ed coaches. To them, all guys were supposed to look like jocks. As a result, the entire staff made me feel quite unwelcome. In response, I basically stopped going to school and only attended fifty-one of the 180 days of school that year. Instead of going to school, I went to my friend's house to smoke pot and play guitar. Then, I'd promptly return home when school was out, as if that's where I'd been all day. I found playing guitar and smoking pot to be much more enjoyable than sitting in school.

The school never reported to my parents that I was missing in action. Because of the hair fiasco, I think they were glad I wasn't showing up. My parents didn't find out I hadn't been attending until the end of the year. By this time, my mom and dad had pretty much given up on me anyway. They knew I had an independent spirit and resisted answering to authority in any form. As far as my dad was concerned, he seemed to be okay with that; he'd been similar at my age. The proverbial apple hadn't fallen far from the tree.

Mom didn't seem that concerned either. She had five other kids to worry about, so I don't think she even noticed I was absent most of the time. They felt secure in knowing that, even though I was young, I could take care of myself just fine. Which I could . . . most of the time anyway.

❧

Some of the most memorable moments during this time involved concerts my friends and I attended. I saw Jimi Hendrix twice, Led Zeppelin twice, the Rolling Stones twice, Jethro Tull twice, Deep Purple, Janis Joplin, Jefferson Airplane, Grateful Dead, The Doors, and the list goes on. Seeing all these shows had a huge influence on me musically. And since playing music was my prime directive, it helped tremendously. Unfortunately, this was also a time when my life took an unexpected turn for the worse. It was when I was introduced to the Big H.

Heroin.

In the early summer of 1970, I met some hippies who were about four or five years older than me. Right from the start, I noticed there was something different about them. They had a certain darkness, but I couldn't figure out what it was. They were definitely not the stereotypical peace and love hippie types I was accustomed to. Now, mind you, at this time I was only fifteen, so I was fairly naive and vulnerable when they introduced me to heroin. First, they had me inhale it through my sinuses. Soon after, they injected it directly into my veins. Eventually, I was cooking it up and injecting myself. I did this for a total of four months. But I feel very fortunate that I realized at that young age this was not the direction I wanted my life to go in. So, I decided to get cleaned up. I contacted a friend whose parents owned a cabin in the mountains where we could begin the cleansing. His parents thought we were just going up to hang out at their cabin for a few days, so didn't suspect anything out of the ordinary. But what happened at that cabin was far from ordinary. It turned out to be the most tortuous experience imaginable.

We started the detoxifying process by stripping the bedding and laying a plastic shower curtain over the mattress. Next, I took my clothes off, except for my underwear, and lay on the shower curtain. I then instructed my friend to tie my hands to the bedposts and told him under *no* circumstance should he untie me, no matter how desperately I pleaded.

Then the fun began.

In just a few hours, the withdrawal symptoms came on. Sweating, nausea, trembling, agonizing pain, anxiety, and finally, panic took effect. And it only got worse from there. At about 3:00 a.m., I began throwing up profusely, accompanied by severe diarrhea (hence the shower curtain). The pain from the withdrawals came on strong, drenching me in sweat, and I began shaking uncontrollably.

At that point, my friend thought I was going to die and wanted to rush me to the hospital.

"Absolutely not," I said. I didn't want anyone to know about my problem. And, as it turned out, no one did—until now.

The physical apocalypse lasted another two days before it finally began to subside. My friend had been trying to feed me and give me water the entire time, but nothing would stay in my system for more than a few seconds. I was extremely weak by the time he untied me from the restraints and could barely stand on my own. I later learned I could have easily died from attempting this "cold turkey." But I didn't care. I just wanted it to be over. At the age of fifteen, I was done with drugs.

There was a silver lining to all of this, as I believe there always is. Years later, I felt qualified to educate my students on the subject. I'm sure at some point they'd heard the anti-drug lecture in school or from their parents but hearing it from someone who'd experienced it firsthand may have left a stronger impression. When I discussed the topic, I didn't go into detail about what I'd gone through, but I'm sure they could tell by the seriousness in my tone and my facial expression that this was *not* to be taken lightly. I may have convinced them it was not a road they dare travel. I later learned my advice was influential to some, because they revealed to me how they avoided temptation by heeding my advice. I was very happy to hear of this.

3

Breaking the Chains

Inever did return to school at the end of that summer. I became an eighth-grade dropout. Just two weeks after getting clean from heroin, I decided I wasn't going back. If I continued, it would lead me to a place I didn't like, and I would regret that for the rest of my life. I had no use for what they taught within the confines of those walls. Those things were for other people, not for me. To me, they meant nothing, they were just a distraction from where I needed to focus.

It was also at this time that another tragedy occurred. My guitar hero, Jimi Hendrix, died from asphyxiation caused by a mixture of drugs and alcohol on September 18, 1970. He was only twenty-seven. It was my mom who came into my room that morning to tell me. She was noticeably upset because she knew how the news was going to affect me. She was right, I was devastated. First, it was my friend, Jerry, and now, my guitar hero, Jimi.

On that day, I asked my dad to take me to the local music store so I could trade my bass in for a Fender Stratocaster guitar, the same kind Jimi played. The rest is history. I never looked back. I was surprised Dad would do this, given all the trouble I'd put him through over the years, but I think he understood my passion because he had always wanted to be a performer. He bought me an old beat-up acoustic guitar when I pleaded for him to get one after seeing the Beatles on the Ed Sullivan Show back in 1964. He used to pick it up and strum it while singing along with Johnny Cash, Charlie Pride, Hank Williams, and Merle Haggard. This was usually after a few beers, so he was a bit out of pitch and missing the beat. But nonetheless, he had fun. Mom sometimes sang along with him, but after my dad had a few more beers, she would just shake her head and retreat to the kitchen.

I thought it was hilarious.

At the time of Jimi's death, I informed Dad of my decision to not return to school. He was disappointed but understood that I was determined to follow my dream. There was nothing he could do to persuade me otherwise, and he knew it. Besides, he'd left school in the eighth grade too. And Mom was pulled out of school in the eighth grade to help her stepmother run a daycare center. So, it kind of ran in the family.

Dad told me he was okay with my decision, but he wouldn't provide food and shelter for me if I wasn't going to school, which made perfect sense. I asked him if I could borrow the ten-man tent we used for camping.

"You can have that old tent," he replied. "We haven't used it in years."

I thought, *Great, I have a home. Now I just need a place to set it up.* Thankfully, this turned out to be an easy task to achieve.

My friend James lived on the opposite side of town with his mom who owned a vacant lot next to their house, and said I was welcome to pitch the tent there. The only problem was that the entire lot was overgrown with sticker bushes. To remedy this, I used a machete to cut a trail to the middle, then cut and leveled out an area to put up my new "home." After setting it up, I ran a long extension cord from their house to the tent for electricity, which provided power for my heater, lamp, portable record player, and, most importantly, my guitar amp. For sleeping, I had a cot with a thin mattress topped with a sleeping bag. This was the life. At the age of fifteen, I considered it quite cool to have my own place. Being independent for the first time in my life was an incredibly eye-opening experience. The feeling of this newfound freedom was exhilarating. I was intoxicated with the thought that everything from this point on would be the result of my own choices. And those choices were limitless. My first and foremost objective was to wholly dedicate myself to playing guitar. When I wasn't playing, I read books on philosophy, metaphysics, psychology, and spirituality. You know, all the things I wanted to learn that weren't taught in school, reaffirming the idea that quitting was the best choice.

With this newfound freedom and this luxurious new lifestyle, there were a few problems that arose. First, the spiders living in the stickers really enjoyed my comfy little abode as much, if not more, than I. To my disapproval, they all decided to move in and become my roommates. This did not bode well with me at all. I freaking *hate* spiders! There were times I woke up in the middle of the night or early morning only to find a huge brown recluse running up my sleeping bag directly toward my head. I'd jump up with a yelp, throw my sleeping bag off, and then frantically search for the spider who almost ate my face. Of course, I could never find it, which made it nearly impossible to go back to sleep. I had nightmares about those dreadful creatures for years after. I may have developed a bit of a phobia because of those "joyful" little arachnid encounters.

The second problem I ran into was snow. That winter, an overabundance fell. I set my alarm to go off every two hours so I could shovel the snow off the tent. Otherwise, it would start to cave in. But I didn't complain. After all, it was my decision to put myself in this situation. Besides, I was quite content because I could play guitar as much as I liked.

I carried on a daily routine of learning songs by ear from records and found myself getting better day by day. Initially, I was very shy about playing in front of people. So, many of my friends didn't even know I played and were quite impressed when I eventually got up the nerve to play for them.

For income, I found a job at a stereo shop just a couple of miles from my fabric mansion. I made a whopping $1.25 an hour. Woo hoo! But I didn't need much, as there was no rent, or telephone and electricity bills to pay. I rode my bike to work and paid my landlord—Jim's mom—a dollar per day for breakfast and dinner, and my boss usually bought me lunch. I was set.

While working there, I learned how to build speaker cabinets from the ground up. This included cutting the baffle boards, routing speaker holes, staining the wood, connecting the speakers, and wiring crossovers. I gained a vast amount of knowledge regarding acoustics and sound distribution. It was the perfect job for an up-and-coming musician.

Then came a day when it all abruptly ended. I was working the table saw to cut two hundred baffle boards—the front boards where speakers are mounted—out of 4-foot by 8-foot, 3/4-inch particle board. After about three hours, I started to become disoriented and a bit dizzy from the monotony of repetition and the loud, continuous noise from the saw. I looked down to see the blade of the saw between the second and third fingers of my right hand. I literally felt the air current from the blade between my fingers.

I immediately jerked my hands away from the board, causing it to fly up and hit me in the forehead, knocking me to the floor and then landing on top of me. I pushed the board off, got up, turned off the saw, and started shaking uncontrollably, drenched in sweat from trauma. After several minutes, I knew I couldn't go back to the table saw. I was still shaking. So, I decided to do something a little safer, like routing out the speaker holes in the baffle boards I'd already cut. Which, as it turned out, wasn't much safer.

The router itself had a heavy engine on top with a sharp drill bit on the underside to cut the speaker holes. It was very difficult to maneuver because of the top-heavy weight distribution. I'd been cutting for about two hours when the bit suddenly broke, throwing the router off balance with the remainder of the bit catching my T-shirt and pulling the drill toward me. If that bit made contact, it would cut me up like salami, so I immediately jerked the router's power cable from the wall, stopping it just before it sliced into me.

On that day, after almost severing two fingers and nearly being eaten by a ravenous machine, I decided it was time for a career change, something perhaps a little less hazardous. Luckily, I found a new job opportunity straight away: selling marijuana.

From my previous employment, I'd saved enough money to invest in this exciting new enterprise. But being a teenage pot dealer didn't really pan out the way I'd hoped. It all went up in smoke. Literally. My friends and I ended up smoking more than I was selling, which didn't turn much of a profit. Now, I know I mentioned earlier that I was finished with drugs, but pot is not a drug, it's an herb. (There's always a loophole.) I quickly stopped selling the herb and applied for any odd jobs that came along. These involved landscaping, painting houses, building rockeries, picking strawberries, cleaning garages, laying foundations, carpentry, and so on. I wasn't making enough to put into a 401(k) by any means, but I was getting by.

On one occasion, while at the grocery store buying lunch supplies before heading to a job, I realized I didn't have enough funds to buy what I wanted, which was a loaf of bread, bologna, and cheese. So, I slipped the cheese into my coat pocket—and got busted. Of course! It's why I was never suited for a life of crime; I couldn't do anything without getting caught.

My punishment for this high crime was one year of probation, and I had to build a new porch for the back entrance to the police station. The porch is still there, but now the station is a Veterans of Foreign Wars (VFW) Hall. I guess I can add to my list of odd job skills that I build porches as well—but only if I'm caught doing something stupid.

Around this time, my luxurious abode, Casa de Cloth, started getting moldy and was beginning to fall apart. Fortunately, my friend's mom, who owned the property, offered me their basement to reside in.

I thought that was a very nice gesture—until I moved in. If I thought the spider situation in my tent was bad, the situation in the basement was far worse! It was a breeding ground for these beastly little vampires. I had to saturate the place with insecticide every couple of days, but this only seemed to piss them off, encouraging them to multiply more vigorously. One day, when I came home after working a job, the little bastards had woven a web from my guitar neck to the lamp. I thought, *Is nothing sacred?*

When I moved into the basement, I also acquired a new responsibility; I had to take care of their elderly German Shepard, Lucy. She was no longer allowed in the main part of the house because the poor thing had lost the use of her hind legs and couldn't control her bowels, which made life much more interesting for me. The basement entrance was outside the house, so to take Lucy outside, I would have to lift her hind legs and walk her up the stairs like a wheelbarrow. Each time, I hoped she wouldn't lose control of her bowels and share her insides on my shoes. This only worked occasionally; most of the time, I would have to hose her excrement off my patent leathers and down the basement drain.

So, there I was, living in a dark, damp arachnid factory, getting bitten every night, with a poor old, crippled dog as a roommate who couldn't control her bowels. Life was good.

During this time, some of my fondest memories came from attending outdoor music festivals. The only problem was, my friends and I were tired of trying to find transportation or hitchhike to these events. So, to alleviate the problem, I purchased a 1961 Ford Econoline van from a junkyard sale for two hundred bucks. The van actually worked. Kinda. And even though I wasn't old enough to drive, I now owned a vehicle, and drove anyway.

Following rules was not my forte.

One concert that really stood out from the others was The Seattle Pop Festival, headlined by The Doors I drove my van to the event with a couple of friends and arrived early. About halfway through the day, one of my friends asked to borrow the van to make a beer run. Even though he was only a couple of years older than me, he looked twenty-one and had a fake ID, so he always succeeded. He returned about four hours later without the beer he supposedly went to get. Naturally, I was suspicious as to his whereabouts while he was parading around in my van, but I wasn't about to let it ruin the day.

The Doors were two hours late getting on stage, and by that time, Jim Morrison was way too drunk to perform. The roadies had to keep picking him up on stage, but he'd only make a few ill attempts at singing before taking a few steps sideways and falling again. Although I found this to be quite entertaining, I really wanted to hear a few songs. Once my friends and I realized there was no way this was going to happen, we decided to make our departure.

When we got back to the van, I spotted a few older guys I didn't know sitting in the back, smoking pot and surrounded by TVs. I thought, *Something's not right with this picture.*

Duh!

My friend explained that he and his new friends had gone on a little house-raiding safari when he borrowed the van. Clearly, I was not pleased. I yelled at them to get out and take their stolen TVs with them. This didn't go over very well. Two of the guys jumped me, slammed me to the ground, and started punching me in the face, giving me a bloody nose and a black eye. So, it became apparent that I was unwillingly elected to transport these derelicts, along with their arsenal of stolen TVs out of the fairgrounds.

Oh, boy.

As we pulled out from the parking lot into the miles-long post-concert traffic, I smelled gasoline. The engine then started to choke, then stalled. I restarted it, revving the engine so it wouldn't die again. The smell of gasoline grew worse, and the engine began to overheat because of the constant revving, all the while still stuck at a standstill in traffic. Suddenly, the engine burst into flames.

Not a good scenario. The engine was located between the two front bucket seats. To make things worse, the driver's door wouldn't open because a previous accident had smashed it in. I was stuck. I did, however, manage to escape by jumping over the flames to the passenger seat and out the door, burning my hair, eyebrows, and arm hairs in the process.

The culprits who stole the TVs scurried off into the night like the little rodents they were. My remaining friend and I found a place to sit on someone's front lawn adjacent to the inferno.

So there I was, sitting in some stranger's yard with singed hair, eyebrows, and arm hairs, a bloody nose, and a black eye watching my new van with hot TVs inside go up in flames. I thought, *Now is the perfect time to fire up a joint.* So, I did just that.

4

Six-String Fever

For me, the '70s were a decade of determination, enlightenment, and adventure, along with an abundance of mishaps. At the beginning of the '70s, I became very serious about my commitment to guitar. I played constantly. If I wasn't practicing, I was jamming with friends.

But there was one thing missing: a location to jam. The tiny basement with the arachnid vampires and the poopy dog wasn't going to cut it. So, I searched around and found a tiny house for rent at the back of a church parking lot. The rent was only forty dollars per month, which was perfect for a musician's budget.

Over the next two years, we jammed and smoked until the wee hours almost every night of the week. We named our little jamming project "Yellow Dog" after the hippie comic book of the same name. The local police department paid numerous visits and became so familiar with our *high* jinks that they didn't even bother knocking when they paid us a visit in response to a noise complaint. We were so loud we wouldn't have heard them anyway.

When they opened the door, we would stop playing and stare at them with bloodshot eyes and Cheshire smiles. Pot smoke would billow out the opened door and into their nostrils as they peered down at my coffee table strewn with a multitude of smokeable herbage and paraphernalia. They eventually gave up mentioning anything about the pot. They knew it was pointless. I think they figured that as long as we were all in one place and staying out of trouble, it made their job easier.

At times, they would stick around to listen to a few tunes. They probably received a bit of a contact high from the noxious cloud permeating the room because they would always depart with sheepish grins that weren't there upon their arrival. Bless their hearts.

In the early part of the decade, I attended several concerts for musical inspiration. One such concert was Beck, Bogart, and Appice. Since Jeff Beck was such a huge influence on my playing, I couldn't imagine missing the show. I arrived early to the Paramount Theater in downtown Seattle that night to witness Beck's madman guitar aerobics. The show went great until Jeff's amp started cutting out. He became so frustrated he took off his white Stratocaster guitar, hurled it across the stage, and stormed off. We were unsure whether he would return to finish the set. Eventually, the crew fixed the issue, and he took to the stage again. Thankfully.

When the show was over, my friend Dave and I decided to stick around by the backstage entrance to see if I could get a guitar pick. The weather conditions were not good. It was cold and pouring rain, but my friend and I braved the elements, soaked and shivering. We noticed one limo remained and figured it had to be Jeff's since the other band members had already left in another. He eventually showed up at the backstage door arguing with someone who I suspected was his tour manager.

After they finished bickering, Jeff started making his way toward the limo. I thought it probably wasn't the best time to be asking for a pick, but Dave insisted and pushed me toward Jeff. So, I nervously went up and asked for a pick.

At first, I thought he was going to punch me. Then he must have realized that I'd been waiting there in the rain, shivering my ass off for this one chance. He opened the limo door. "Get in, mate."

Really? I thought.

"So, my friend, you've been standing out here in the rainy cold just to get a bloody guitar pick?" he asked.

"Yup," I replied.

He reached into his Pan Am flight bag, dug out a Herco Heavy pick, and handed it to me.

I was in heaven!

Jeff smiled, shook my hand, and patted me on the back. "You've got determination," he said. "You're gonna do great, kid."

I took that guitar pick and played with it exclusively until it was worn down to a nub. Inevitably, it became unusable. For years, I carried that nub with me in the hip pocket of my jeans as a good luck charm.

Fast forward fifteen years to 1985. I was backstage at a National Association of Music Merchants show (NAMM) when I happened to run into Jeff again. Roger Fisher, the guitarist from Heart, was also there showing Jeff a new guitar he'd just designed. Jeff had a broken thumb so couldn't do much with it.

He handed it to me.

Yikes!

I started doodling around with some of my two-handed technique (which I'll elaborate on later).

"That's really cool, mate," Jeff said.

I then introduced myself.

"I know who you are," he said. "You're that bloke who does all that two-handed stuff like you were just playing. It's brilliant!"

Naturally, I was on cloud nine hearing this.

I then told him the story about our meeting outside the Paramount Theater in Seattle fifteen years earlier.

"You're that kid who was standing in the rain freezing your arse off waiting to get a guitar pick from me," he said.

"Yup, that was me." I reached into my hip pocket and pulled out that nub of what was once his guitar pick and handed it to him.

He looked at it and then me. "So, this is it?"

"What's left of it."

We both laughed. I told him how much it meant to me that he took a couple of moments that night to be so kind to a soaking-wet young guitarist with big dreams. His actions helped inspire me to become what I had.

"Now I'm giving this gift back to you," I said. "Thank you."

Jeff looked very moved by this. I don't think there was a dry eye in the room at that moment. To this day, I have *never* turned down taking a picture, signing an autograph, or giving a guitar pick to a fan, and I never will. I know the true value of such gestures.

When I reminisce back to the early '70s, I remember that, aside from my guitar addiction, I had become very interested in spiritualism and philosophy. I spent as much time reading as I did practicing. As mentioned previously, I found it to be more advantageous than school academia. Living on my own and learning only what interested me set the agenda for what was to come, and for who I would become. I read books by authors such as Herman Hesse, Aldous Huxley, George Orwell, Ayn Rand, Kahlil Gibran, and studied philosophers such as Ralph Waldo Emerson, Henry David Thoreau, Walt Whitman, and Friedrich Nietzsche.

The material was by no means easy reading. I always had a dictionary and thesaurus by my side to comprehend the terms and ideas I struggled to understand.

Those early days of delving into literature so fraught with intellectual perspectives introduced me to a whole new world. I became a huge fan of deep thinkers. But it wasn't only the books. It was the people I found myself conversing with as well. Friends who were attending college, and even a couple of university professors, took notice of my passion for Eastern and Western philosophy and were more than happy to share their insights. I treasured their intellectual input and mentally inhaled it like a cerebral bong. The in-depth discussions we had while I was between the ages of sixteen and eighteen undoubtedly played a major role in my mental and spiritual development. And for that, I am eternally grateful.

Along the way, there were numerous obstacles that hindered my growth. For instance, a war. Imagine this: it's 1973, I'm eighteen, not in school, and the government wants to ship my ass off to Vietnam.

I don't think so.

Older friends who had gone to Nam and made it back alive were irreparably damaged, either physically or mentally, in some cases, both. They all said, "Don't go." So, I heeded their warning. I, along with a few friends who were in the same situation, devised an escape plan. A mutual friend of ours owned a Volkswagen bus and was more than willing to help us get across the US–Canadian border. At that time, it was about the only way to avoid the draft, other than being in college or having a mental or physical disability. But to my good fortune, right after I turned eighteen, Nixon called off the draft. Needless to say, my friends and I were incredibly relieved.

Years later, I found out the supposed "reason" the US engaged in war with North Vietnam was a complete fabrication by the Pentagon and Robert McNamara, the Secretary of Defense under Lyndon B. Johnson. The story they put forth about the USS Maddox being sunk in the Gulf of Tonkin never happened.[1] There was an altercation between North Vietnamese torpedo boats and the USS Maddox, but the Maddox itself only received one bullet hole. The rest was propaganda aimed at gathering support for the war from the American public. As a result, 58,000 US soldiers were killed.[2] More than 150,000 wounded,[3] not to mention the vast numbers who suffered from post-traumatic stress

---

1   Lieutenant Commander Pat Paterson, U.S. Navy, "The Truth About Tonkin," U.S. Naval Institute, February 2008, https://www.usni.org/magazines/naval-history-magazine/2008/february/truth-about-tonkin.

2   Lieutenant Commander Pat Paterson, U.S. Navy, "The Truth About Tonkin."

3   "Vietnam War Casualties [1955–1975]" The Military Factory, accessed July 9, 2024, Vietnam War Casualties (1955-1975) (militaryfactory.com).

disorder (PTSD), addiction, and other mental health issues, as well as two million Vietnamese killed.[4] All because of a lie to get us into this horrific campaign, which led to financial gain for only a select few. Neither the US nor the Viet Cong won. The only winners were the war profiteers—if you wish to call that winning.

❧

Now, here is an interesting story of what could be considered a "six degrees of separation" incident that ended up being only two degrees of separation from my perspective. It happened one night after a Rolling Stones concert in Seattle. I ran into Leslie Rule, a friend of mine I'd known since junior high who is now a well known author.

That night, Leslie's mother was working nearby at a suicide hotline center. On her break, she picked up Leslie with her two friends from the concert and brought them back to work until her shift was over. During Leslie's stay at the workplace, she met one of her mom's male coworkers, who she described as very peculiar. But her young girlfriends saw him as a well-mannered, soft-spoken gentleman, and thought he was really cute.

Little did these impressionable fourteen-year-old girls know this man was as evil as they come. His name? Ted Bundy. Of course, this was well before he became known as the infamous serial killer. Ann Rule, Leslie's mom, worked with him for some time and thought of him as a handsome, intelligent, and charming man. Ann eventually wrote *The Stranger Beside Me*, a huge bestseller released in 1980 that told about her friendship and experiences working with him. Just recently, Leslie told me the whole story about that night. I can't express how thankful I am that Leslie, her friends, or her mom didn't become unwitting victims of this monster.

---

4 "Vietnam War," history.com, accessed July 9, 2024, https://www.history.com/topics/vietnam-war/vietnam-war-history.

Here is another two-degrees of separation story, one that has a slightly different twist. It happened in 1973 at the Jimi Hendrix Memorial at Eagles Auditorium in Seattle. While I was watching some well-known musicians perform Hendrix songs, I bumped into a small Black man. We smiled at each other and started chatting. He told me he worked as a gardener, then proceeded to tell me all these things about Jimi I didn't know. He said when Jimi was a young boy, he used to practice on a broom to emulate blues and R&B players of the time. Jimi would sit on the floor at the end of his bed each night and play 45 rpm singles over and over until he fell asleep, leaving little pieces of straw scattered around him from strumming the broom.

This polite man then informed me that Jimi finally received an actual guitar as a present one day and that, from that point on, they were inseparable. I continued chatting with this pleasant gentleman for a while longer and then curiously asked who he was and how he knew so much about Jimi.

"I'm Al, Jimi's father," he replied.

I immediately teared up, grabbed him, and gave him a big hug. At this point, he was tearing up too. I shared my condolences regarding the loss of his beloved son and told him I'd seen Jimi perform only months prior to his passing, and how much it had affected me. I also told him I traded in my bass guitar for a Stratocaster on that fateful day, September 18, 1970, and had become a dedicated guitar player because of his son.

He then looked up at me and smiled again, with tears still in his eyes. "Thank you. Thank you so much for that," he said. "It warms my heart to hear someone share how much they were affected by my son."

We then shook hands, gave each other another hug, and parted ways.

That memory will forever be in my heart. Thank you, Al, and thank you, Jimi.

5

The Road to Wonderland

In 1973, at the age of eighteen, I got my feet wet playing live with my first professional band, Outlawd. With my friend Billy Ray at the helm on vocals, we put the band together and set our sights on live performances. Now, when you're eighteen and playing clubs that only allow people twenty-one years of age and over inside, you're permitted to play on stage, but you have to wait outside during breaks. That wasn't much fun during wintertime. I would freeze my butt off behind the club, and my hands grew so numb that by the time I got back inside, I'd have to figure out innovative ways to thaw my fingers before they would function again. Regardless, I had some great times in those formative years, and it gave me the experience I needed to perform live professionally.

꙳

My next musical enterprise was with a group called The Ross Taylor Band. There was no Ross Taylor; we just wanted to have a fictional name, like the band Jethro Tull, though we later learned Jethro Tull was an actual historical figure. Which meant, out of our own stupidity, we were stuck with a name that meant absolutely nothing.

Our first show took place at a logging camp in the Yukon Territory of Canada. Crossing the border from the US into Canada was no easy feat, especially when you have a bunch of longhairs smelling like pot in a 1951 Chevy panel truck filled with instruments. Oh, no, this wasn't going to be a walk in the park. And sure enough, as soon as the border patrol saw our mangy asses, he made us pull over and unload all our gear, got the drug-sniffing dogs out, drilled us with questions for two hours, and made us write down every piece of equipment, including serial numbers and the value of each. It took about four hours before we were finally back on the road again. We thought we'd be welcomed into Canada by Rocky and Bullwinkle, but, as it turned out, it was Boris and Natasha.

After driving six hours north from the border, we came to the dirt-road turn-off for the logging camp. Now, GPS didn't exist in 1974, so our only way to navigate was with written directions and a crinkly old road map. It was a miracle we even found that dirt road in the middle of nowhere in the dark. That was when the real adventure began. It was a twenty-mile drive through the mountains in the snow with bald tires and a five-hundred-foot cliff at our side. Which, if we'd happened to drive off, would surely have been our demise, and that old charcoal-colored '51 Chevy would have become our eternal sarcophagus.

After a two-and-a-half-hour drive on that suicidal roadway, we arrived at our destination. All of us were more than a bit tattered and had lost a good portion of tooth enamel from grinding our teeth while on that treacherous route. When we found our disgruntled host, he escorted us to the "elegant" suite they'd prepared for us: a wood cabin with no insulation, a potbellied stove for heat, and five cots. Yup, this was the high life.

When we awoke the next day, we got coffee from the cafeteria and went to the bar to set up our gear. The supposed stage looked frightful. It was a rectangular box about two feet high with only enough room for the drums and was enclosed in metal bars and chicken wire.

Huh?

That night, when we entered the stage cage for our first set, the proprietor quickly fastened a paddle lock outside the entry door. We inquired what it was for.

"It's for your safety," he replied. A short time later, we found out why this was considered a necessity.

It was a tradition for these loggers—or hairy Neanderthals, I'm not sure—to ingest sizable dosages of mescaline while consuming shots of Wild Turkey whiskey, chasing that with buckets of lager. I guess this was considered the norm for Saturday night festivities. Then the excitement began. As we performed on stage dressed up like a transvestite troupe, the gorillas in the mist (of smoke) ogled us like they might get lucky—NOT a comforting thought! We were glad to be locked in that cage while the pre-hominid Yukon Jacks were kept on the outside.

As the evening progressed, the powerful hallucinogens and potent libations started to reveal their effect on the barbarians, who began throwing chairs, tables, and bottles at us as we played their favorite songs. At this time, with the cage shaking and glass breaking all around us, we decided it best to skip the ballads. We had only played two sets when the owner unlocked the cage and ordered us to pack up our gear and get the hell out of there. We delightfully obliged.

Our trip back down the mountain was much more pleasant than the trip up. We were pleased with the early departure and discussed what a horrendously scary gig it had become. So, from the hellish crossing at the border to driving eight hours with an old, wrinkled map as our only guide, to pivoting our bald-tire van up a snowy mountainous suicidal thoroughfare, to sleeping on cots in a frozen shed and playing for a room full of drunken hallucinating Sasquatches, this was a gig to remember. But in the end, we were happy: we made $350!

Collectively, that is, not individually.

Shortly after that gig, we had another one in Missoula, Montana, at a place called The Trading Post. This was a very popular venue for Pacific Northwest bands, and we were more than excited to have a show booked there. This establishment had an actual stage, a dance floor—and women. Wow! Far cry from our previous engagement with the all-male logging primates.

Halfway through the show, during our second break, an attractive brunette approached and we began chatting it up. At the end of the night she asked if I'd like to come over to her place to finish off a bottle of Jack Daniels.

Hmmm, let me think about that . . . Okay!

We spent a wonderful night together drinking, laughing, and, well—you know. The following afternoon, as we lay passed out in the back bedroom of her single-wide, I heard a pounding on the front door accompanied by a burly voice yelling: "Trish, open the fucking door!"

As she lay there in a deep slumber, I went up to the door and saw the deadbolt was fastened, so I peered through the door curtains to investigate. What I saw next horrified me. It was a belt buckle. This guy must have been as tall as the trailer itself. I rushed back and shook Trish awake as the pounding and yelling continued. When she awoke, she panicked and let out a little squeal with a facial expression of sheer terror. She then informed me it was her husband.

Oh, shit! I thought, then whispered, "You never told me you were married!"

"You never asked. And besides, he wasn't supposed to be back until tomorrow!" she replied.

How does that matter now? I wondered. Then I heard him try to break in the door and dreaded what was about to transpire.

Unfortunately, the trailer home had those little slat windows you have to crank open, so I couldn't just open the window and jump out. I ran back to the bedroom, got my clothes, then grabbed a chair in the dining area and threw it through the slatted window. Glass shattered everywhere as I jumped out and cut my foot on the shards below. I ran as if my life depended on it, which it most assuredly did. So, there I was, severely hungover, running butt-ass naked with a bloody foot through the snow with clothes and boots in tow, being chased by Paul Bunyan into an endless forest. (I had a feeling my epitaph would read something of this nature.)

Luckily, my skinny ass could outrun Paul, or whatever his name was. When I reached the woods, I got dressed, made my way back to the highway, and hitchhiked back to town, fearing all the while I might run into the behemoth woodsman.

❧

Another little episode happened when I was performing with Silverlode, the last group I was in from the Seattle area. We were playing a packed biker bar just south of Tacoma, Washington. The bikers were totally inebriated, as is usually the case. A squirrely little squinty-eyed biker with long, greasy hair and a scraggly beard kept coming up to me between songs demanding we play "Johnny B. Goode." I explained it wasn't on our set list, and that we'd never played it together. This didn't work for him. He was pissed. Later that night, he stumbled up to me while on stage and pulled out a Colt.45, pointed it at my head, cocked the trigger, and said, "Play 'Johnny B. Goode,' you fuck face!" So, I counted off: 1-2-3 and played: da-da-da-dadadadada. The rest of the band followed suit, and we played it perfectly from beginning to end. I guess we were miraculously inspired by this gentleman's "kind" request.

❧

On another occasion in 1976, another slice of lunacy pie was served while Silverlode played a gig in Boseman, Montana, at a place called Molly Browns. While on break I was sitting at a table drinking my usual 7UP when this psycho-sorceress dominatrix *came up and* sat down across from me. With hair every color of the spectrum and sticking out in all directions, she looked as though she'd recently fallen victim to a lightning strike. She was draped in jet-black clothes with shiny little sparkles dusted all about. Tattoos of skulls, demons and pentagrams covered her arms, and she wore lace-up boots that might have been hand-crafted in the 1600s by the witches of Salem themselves.

I noticed right away that she seemed to be in an alternate state-of-being: she glared at me with her solid black pupils, likely tripping on some mind-warping hallucinogen. With her eyes seemingly throwing daggers at me, she leaned in close with breath that smelled as if she'd just snacked on a carcass and whispered, "My name is Sin, and I want to eat you,"

I knew right then I wouldn't be bringing this one home to meet Mom.

Now, how is it that I am the only one who could summon the one demon-witch in the whole state of Montana? What are the odds? Anyway, I got back on stage with my 7UP, and we proceeded to play our last set. About halfway through, I got this eerie feeling something was a bit off, yet it was a strangely familiar sensation.

Uh oh.

Realization dawned. I'd been slipped a psychedelic mickey. The only one who could've done it was the wicked demon-witch.

As the powerful hallucinogen increasingly grew stronger and stronger, the neck of my guitar began moving around like a snake. I had no idea what song we were playing. I informed the band that I'd been slipped a mickey and was having difficulty staying in the same dimension. When we reached the last song, they asked if I was able to finish, but I just stood there staring at them with dilated pupils the size of olive pits and a crooked grin, unable to respond. The singer said goodnight to the crowd and the band left the stage.

Everyone but me, that is. I just stood there in la-la land with my stupid-ass grin and black pupils.

The next thing I knew, we were back at the hotel. I had no clue how we got there, it just happened. As I lay on my bed, drifting in a sea of hallucinations, the phone suddenly rang. I picked it up.

"How ya feelin', Stevie?" responded a raspy voice.

It was the demon-witch, the last person in the world I wanted to hear from!

She informed me she was going to come snatch me up and take me back to her place so we could roller skate in her living room . . . wearing nothing but overcoats, ski masks, and goggles.

I quickly hung up the phone and covered my head with the blanket. Thankfully, she never showed up. As my band mates and I left town the next morning, I kept looking behind me to see if the demon-witch was following—perhaps on a broom.

At this point in my life, I was getting a bit frustrated playing Top 40 clubs. I saw no future in it, nor money. To a degree, I felt my fellow band members had similar thoughts. It was frustrating because I wasn't earning enough playing music to make a living. It was obvious I needed to make a change.

In late 1977, while playing our last show of the tour in Billings, Montana, I called the music store in West Seattle to schedule more lessons with my teacher, Don Mock. At that time, he was considered to be one of the top jazz and fusion players as well as the best teacher in Seattle. But when I called, they said he was no longer there. He'd moved to Hollywood, California, to teach at a new guitar school called the Guitar Institute of Technology.

"What? A guitar school?" I responded loudly.

The music store didn't have the number for the school, so I called directory assistance in Hollywood. To my amazement, they found it under new listings! I called the number and a lady answered. I asked if Don Mock was available, to which she replied, "Let me go check to see if he's teaching a class."

I was holding the phone anxiously waiting when a voice came on and said, "Hello?" I recognized it right away. I was so excited to hear about the school, but Don wouldn't elaborate. Instead, all he said was, "Lynch, quit your band, sell your gear, and get your ass down here!"

And just a few short months later, I was there.

6

The Best Decision Ever

The decision to attend the Guitar Institute of Technology in early 1978 was the single most important decision I could've made for my music career. It became a monumental turning point in my life. Even though I was an enthusiastic and dedicated player before attending the Guitar Institute, the school inspired me to the point of obsession about perfecting my skill. Not only did the courses teach the theory needed to achieve this, but they also provided all the materials needed to become a true professional. This included writing, composing, studio sessions, live performances, teaching, and how to connect with studios, venues, other musicians, and so on. The institute taught classical, blues, and rock, but their main focus was jazz.

And that's what piqued my interest. I wanted to learn the theory behind jazz and how musicians created their incredibly innovative and melodic solos. I figured this would inspire me to experiment outside the typical blues/rock phrases dominating the rock genre, and it most certainly did. I dedicated myself to learning how to incorporate a variety of jazz phrases into common rock chord progressions. This helped cultivate a more unique playing style for the years to come. Don Mock was instrumental to that shift. I am indebted to him for changing the course of my life—and in a very positive manner I might add. Thank you, my friend.

But let's get back to where this new venture started. It began with my good friend Barry driving me from Seattle down to Hollywood—5858 Hollywood Boulevard, to be exact. We loaded his old Ford pickup truck with my few belongings and began the 1,200-mile trek, stopping only for gas and food. Approaching LA, we drove over the Tejon Pass (also known as The Grapevine), a sea of lights as far as the eye could see appeared on the horizon. Neither of us had ever witnessed such a spectacle. At 4,400 feet in elevation, we had a mind-blowing view of an everlasting, tangled mass of houses, apartments, businesses, and freeways that held sixteen million people! We both stared in silence with our mouths agape as we slowly crept down into this otherworldly neon landscape.

We arrived in Hollywood at 3:00 a.m. We were tired, hungry, burned out, and lost. By the time we finally found the school, my friend was not happy. He just wanted to drop me off and get the hell out of there as quickly as possible. He helped unload my things in front of the school and said, "Good luck with this shit hole." Then he jumped back in his truck and sped away.

So, there I was, standing in front of the Guitar Institute at 4:30 in the morning, completely exhausted, disoriented, hungry, and in an unsafe neighborhood with my Les Paul and Stratocaster guitars, Marshall amplifier, my suitcase, a small mattress, and $200 in my pocket. I just smiled and thought, *Let the adventure begin!*

Around 8:00 a.m., a friendly-looking little lady showed up. She looked up at me and asked who I was. I recognized her voice and told her that I was the former student of Don Mock, who had spoken with her a few months prior and again just a week ago to get directions. Her name was Becky.

"You're Steve, from Seattle," she said.

"Yup," I said with bloodshot eyes and a half-baked smile.

"What are you doing out on the sidewalk with all your stuff? And where's your car?"

I told her I didn't have a car and that the friend who dropped me off wanted to get the hell out of there, so he left me on the sidewalk with my possessions as he angrily fled the scene.

She laughed and said "Come on. I'll give you a hand getting your things inside before you get robbed or killed."

I laughed in response.

"I'm serious!" she said, and we both laughed.

Later that morning, after showing me around the school, Becky told me where I'd be living and gave me the address. I left my belongings at the school and began walking toward my new place of residence about a mile away. As I made my way down Hollywood Boulevard, I saw a variety of characters who appeared to be out of sorts not only with this world, but with whatever world from which they came. There were runaways, drug addicts, thieves, con artists, bikers, drug dealers, prostitutes, and others I didn't even know how to describe . . . perhaps from another dimension?

So this is my new home. How exciting! I thought.

❧

A few days after settling into my new abode, classes began. Overwrought with anxiety to get started, I arrived at the school a little early that first day. I took the elevator up to the third floor only to find a hallway full of what appeared to be a mob of deranged misfits wandering about, mumbling to themselves.

Oh, no! I thought. *Is this what I'm going to look like after a few months in this Guitar "Institute?"*

As I stood there holding my guitar case in that corridor of mental disorder, a lady approached. She informed me I'd gotten off on the wrong floor; the Guitar Institute was on the fourth floor.

My shoulders then dropped from my ears, and I got back on the elevator. I was so relieved to find Becky there to explain what had just transpired. She started laughing uncontrollably.

"The third floor is a halfway house for the mentally ill! It prepares them for release back into society again," she told me.

I was quite relieved they released *me*. If I were them, I probably wouldn't have.

After getting accustomed to the school schedule, I found myself practicing eight hours a day in addition to the five hours of classes. Obviously, I wasn't getting much sleep, but my playing was improving dramatically. Everything they were handing out in class I feverishly tried to conquer. I formed blisters, then the blisters turned to calluses, then the calluses would fall off, and then the whole process would repeat itself, over and over. I didn't mind. Seeing the improvement in my playing was well worth the effort and the pain.

During this repetition, I practiced with complete privacy in a little room at the back of the school. I acquired the room in exchange for setting up all the classrooms for the next day's lessons and making photocopies for each class. I considered that to be a very generous bargain. The room had a full view of the shimmering lights spreading across the entire LA basin. It was my inspiration and the place where I willfully carried out a relentless routine of practice seven days a week for the duration of the school year. My hands bitched at me the entire time.

I had one issue with the curriculum: most of it was written in musical notation—notes written on a musical staff. It didn't show what the notes looked like on the guitar neck itself, which I found to be very frustrating. I began transcribing the notation to guitar necks I'd sketched out on paper. This enabled me to memorize everything by visualizing the shapes of the scale patterns and chord inversions.

When a couple of teachers noticed my approach, they agreed that it made more sense from a guitarist's perspective. Some asked if they could use it for their classes, which I consented to wholeheartedly. I felt honored they would even ask.

❧

Around the third month in, we had one of our first visiting clinicians, a musician named Emmett Chapman. He invented an instrument called the Chapman Stick, an instrument that resembles a narrow plank of wood but with strings attached. It's held in a manner similar to a guitar but with the neck raised and the base positioned closer to the body. You play it by placing your left hand on a set of five strings, which are in the lower register bass notes. With your right hand, you play on a separate set of five strings, which are in the higher register treble notes. It's similar to playing a piano, except instead of keys triggering a strike pad that hits the strings, your fingers tap the strings directly.

During Emmett's clinic, he mentioned that he used to play guitar with both hands on the fingerboard but wanted to devise an instrument that could accompany him with both lower and higher frequencies. This is how the concept for his creation began.

After the clinic, I approached him and asked if he could demonstrate his two-handed guitar technique for me, the one that inspired the Stick. When he agreed, I handed him my guitar. What I witnessed next blew me away! He played double-scale patterns and chord inversions with both hands all over the neck. The sound was like nothing I had ever heard. I'd already experimented with double-handed playing after learning a few tricks from a Seattle guitarist named Steve Buffington, and by watching blues guitarist Harvey Mandel experiment with it, but I'd never seen anything like what Emmett was doing. His technique with double-handed playing was in a league of its own.

As it turned out, Emmet's clinic changed my perspective of guitar considerably. My approach took a dramatic turn. I immediately started writing down all the scales, intervals, triads, arpeggios, and chord inversions in this two-handed format. I struggled with it for months, because the technique was much more complex to both visualize and play than using only one hand on the fingerboard. I ended up incorporating this technique with everything I learned at the school. The experience gave me a feeling of euphoria. I was creating something different from what anyone else had—in my own way, that is. To create a technique that I could not only incorporate into my playing style but teach to others gave me a huge sense of accomplishment. I remember thinking, *This is the ticket that will allow me to stand apart from the others.*

And, indeed, it did just that.

About halfway through the year, I found there was one teacher who didn't seem to care much for me. I wasn't sure why, but it may have had something to do with the fact I didn't fit the part of a jazz artist. I guess I looked a bit too rock and roll from his viewpoint with my shag haircut, bell-bottom jeans, platform shoes, solid body guitar and black leather coat. If I were a jazzer, I probably wouldn't have liked me either.

This teacher once gave us an assignment to create and perform our own version of a jazz standard. I chose the song, "Stella by Starlight," which was considered a conventional mellow jazz piece—at least until I got hold of it! When I got up to perform it, I had the band play it up-tempo—and hard. I counted it off, and we plowed into a mind-warping heavy metal version of the old classic. Completely untethered. We ended the song with a crescendo of screaming notes and bashing drums befitting a Madison Square Garden finale. The class loved it and responded with cheers and applause. As I stood there with a gleaming smile, as though I'd just finished a sold-out show to 20,000 plus, the teacher glared at me with a look of utter disdain. He put his hand on my shoulder.

"I would like to use Mr. Lynch as an example for all of you," he said to the class.

I thought he was going to say something complimentary regarding the originality of the performance, but it didn't quite play out that way.

"This is *exactly* what I do *NOT* want in my class!" he continued. "Mr. Lynch, please collect your belongings and leave immediately. You are no longer welcome here."

I was in shock, and so were the other students. This was supposed to be an experiment in personal creativity. I guess I crossed the line. I was really bummed-out about the whole thing and felt I'd not only failed the class but my classmates as well. However, I wasn't about to let this incident hamper my curiosity to explore.

Years after this little episode, during the mid-'80s, the Guitar Institute requested I come in for a photo shoot and asked me to bring the gold albums I'd earned with my band as a promotion for the school. I told them I'd be honored and came in for the shoot a couple of days later. While walking down the main hall of the school with my gold records in tow, I ran into a familiar face—the instructor who'd thrown me out of class.

As I walked past, I looked directly at him, grinned, and raised my middle finger just enough for him to notice.

"Touché," he said. (I guess he acknowledged making an example of me that day was perhaps an error on his part).

I just smiled and kept walking. I saw him again after the photo shoot, and we both had a little laugh about the incident.

⚡

One of the most enlightening experiences of my life happened one night when I had the fortunate opportunity to sit with Howard Roberts, the legendary guitarist who wrote the Guitar Institute curriculum. Howard was considered a genius, not only for his uniquely innovative playing style but also for his cutting-edge teaching techniques, which were recognized around the world. He had a reputation for eccentric behavior and a visionary mind. I thought of Howard as a musical Einstein, with a few peculiarities added in.

As we sat in his office that night, we discussed a variety of compelling topics. He found it interesting how I not only understood him, but was able to respond in detail, sharing my own insights and perspectives. We continued our extensive, encyclopedic, esoteric conversation straight through until 8:00 a.m.

During our conversation, he shared a story about living with a friend who collected oddities and books of non-conventional wisdom. This piqued my curiosity, as I was fascinated with alternative, non-conformist knowledge that was not customarily held within typical social circles. This was not the "eating of the forbidden fruit" type of information. On the contrary, it was positive and enlightening. Our discussion was incredibly inspirational for me, both musically and spiritually.

That night made me realize that most artists follow the road less traveled, the one that goes directly to the source, or the "self," for it is the road to their creative destiny. From that point on, my guitar playing, and musical writing became entangled with my spiritual growth. It was magical.

꙳

The students attending the Guitar Institute while I was there were a highly diverse group. They came from various countries with an assortment of personalities and playing styles. Guitar ideas were frequently shared in the hallway, by students and teachers alike, with a complete lack of a competitive mindset or animosity. Everyone was just there to learn. It was the best atmosphere I could've ever imagined for a place of study.

Every now and then, one student, Jennifer Batten, visited the room I practiced in to check in with me and exchange ideas. Sometimes, Jennifer would hear me playing some of the two-handed technique I was working on and tap on the door to inquire about what I was doing, which I was always glad to share. She even had a private lesson with me after we graduated, which I thought was pretty cool. She took the ideas gleaned from our sessions and created her own amazing version of the technique. She later had the incredible opportunity to play guitar for Michael Jackson; it really doesn't get any better than that! After which she toured with one of my biggest influences, Jeff Beck. I couldn't be prouder of what she has become. She's well respected as one of the best female guitarists worldwide.

But I'm unbiased; I think she's one of the best, regardless of gender.

❧

I remember sitting in my practice room in the back of the school with that panoramic view of an endless sea of lights called LA, thinking that maybe one day people would know my name. A few years later, to my amazement, many did. Certainly not on a grandiose scale, but in a way that I appreciated more than I ever could have wished for. I'd earned respect as a guitarist, and that meant everything to me.

All the students in the graduating class of 1979 became successful to some degree or another. I am very proud of them all and am humbled with gratitude to have had the opportunity to not only learn with them, but *from* them too.

❧

On graduation day, to my surprise, I was given the Most Likely to Succeed award, as well as numerous other certificates of merit. I was deeply honored and cherished these accolades. They still hang on my wall to this day, as they always will.

After the awards were handed out, those who wanted to perform at the graduation ceremony were given the opportunity to do so. The song I selected was a jazz standard by Freddie Hubbard called "Little Sunflower." I performed the entire song using both hands on the neck of my guitar, which took most everyone by surprise. There were only a select few who knew I'd been working on the technique throughout the year. When I finished, there was an enthusiastic response from the students and staff, including a standing ovation. I was in disbelief because I wasn't sure how my performance would be received, especially since the last time I had performed at the school I was thrown out of class.

As I left the stage, I was approached by Howard Roberts and studio legend Tommy Tedesco. Both said they were very impressed with my performance and asked if I'd be interested in writing a book about the technique.

"I've been writing all my ideas down since the beginning of the year," I promptly replied. "I have enough material to easily write three books."

"I have a publisher who I think may be interested," Howard said.

I think, at this point, I may have peed myself a little.

A few days later, both Howard and Tommy brought me to their publisher, Dale Zdenek, the owner of Zdenek Publications. I brought several of my handwritten pages, which had circles, squares, and triangles depicting what each hand was playing and the order in which the notes were to be played. I also brought my guitar to demonstrate how to implement the technique. Dale was very excited about what I'd compiled, and within ten minutes, I had a publishing deal!

That pivotal moment encouraged me greatly because I felt it was the first step in establishing myself as a professional in this vast city of artistic virtuosos, where the odds are overwhelmingly stacked against you.

After the release of *The Right Touch* (aptly titled because I use my right hand to touch the strings), the book became an immediate bestseller for Zdenek Publications and remained so for several years, eventually being bought out by Belwin Mills and, later, by Warner Brothers Publications.

7

Life in La-La Land

After graduating from the Guitar Institute and signing a publishing deal, it was time to move into the mainstream. I wanted to embark on some adventures and learn how to navigate the massive place known as the City of Angels, or what I deemed more fitting, the City of Lost Angels.

One humorous incident I'd like to share took place on my way to Chinatown, near downtown LA At the time, I had a beat-up old Plymouth Duster that was painted bright yellow with black stripes running down the middle. Possibly to resemble a bumblebee? I don't know. It didn't quite fit in with the Mercedes, BMWs, Jaguars, Porsches, Range Rovers, or Bentleys, which were the norm for LA, but it was transportation, nonetheless.

On my way to pick up a date one evening, I saw a tall, skinny Black girl hitchhiking on the side of the road. I thought I'd help her out by giving her a lift. Immediately upon entering my bumblebee, she slid right next to me and put her hand on my leg.

"Hi handsome. What's your pleasure?" she asked in a burly voice.

I pulled over so fast I cut off traffic and nearly got plowed into by an oncoming car. I had never encountered anything like this, so wasn't quite sure how to react.

I dealt with it as delicately as possible.

"Get the fuck out of my car!" I yelled, and I immediately felt bad. I mean, what the heck, a "girl's" gotta make a living, right?

Many years later, while watching the movie *Midnight in the Garden of Good and Evil,* I noticed a character who looked strangely familiar. I felt certain it was the transvestite hooker I'd picked up years prior on Hollywood Boulevard.

And what was her character in the movie?

A transvestite hooker. Go figure.

After the short interlude with my new he/she friend, I picked up my flight-attendant date from L.A.X (LA International Airport) and headed for Madam Wong's, a popular club in the middle of Chinatown. That evening, as we were murdering sobriety (in a manner of speaking), I thought it best to leave before becoming too inebriated to drive, so we departed the exquisite establishment.

A couple of blocks down the road, she unexpectedly ripped open her shirt to reveal her humongous breasts, which I was totally fine with. However, it distracted my attention from commandeering the bumblebee just long enough to rear-end a Ford Pinto, known at the time for exploding from rear-end collisions.

Luckily, that didn't happen. But the impact was so forceful it slammed my face into the steering wheel and broke my nose, causing blood to gush everywhere. My date banged her head on the dashboard but was otherwise uninjured.

I didn't understand why she got so upset. After all, it was partially her fault; it was her idea to whip out her wallabies while I was driving, causing me to react like a deer in the boob-lights, thus resulting in the collision. She jumped out of the car and proceeded to scream at me, calling me every name in the book.

As I was trying to calm her down, the police showed up. Oh, boy. So there we were, wasted, standing on the sidewalk, her massive Jehovahs flopping all about while she belted out an unrelenting rant as I stood there in a blood-soaked white shirt next to a dead bumblebee whose face was planted into the ass of a Pinto, all the while being cheered on by homeless people. A lovely sight to behold. At least I knew where I'd be spending the night: jail.

Luckily, Bubba the Buick wasn't in the cage they put me in.

And here is yet another interesting story from around that time while still living in Hollywood. I used to walk by the Scientology building on the corner of Hollywood Boulevard and Highland Avenue. Scientologists often stood in front of the building handing out fliers advertising a free personality test. I ignored them for months but eventually decided to give it a try. Why not? It was free, so I could afford it.

I took the test and answered all the questions as truthfully as possible. After the test, they scheduled me for a follow-up evaluation a few days later. When I went in for the evaluation, they told me I had several flaws in my personality and described each in detail. I had no idea there were so many things wrong with me. I considered myself to be a reasonably sane and logical individual. But they disagreed and said I was in dire need of psychological counseling.

I didn't know anything about the "institution" of Scientology, so I took their analysis seriously. As a result, I became distraught and fell into a bit of a depression. I recall thinking, *I feel normal, so how can there be so many issues mentally?* I lost sleep over it and couldn't concentrate or even eat at times. It wasn't until a few months later that I realized their true intent.

As I walked past the building some time later, I noticed there were different Scientologists handing out fliers, so I decided to retake the test. Except this time, I answered the questions opposite to the way I had previously. After finishing the test, they scheduled me for a follow-up evaluation, the same as before. When I returned for the results, I was surprised to hear the exact same words spoken to me after the first analysis.

I was pissed. I told the guy doing the evaluation that I'd taken the same test a few months earlier, answering the questions opposite from the way I did this time, but the results turned out exactly the same. He didn't know how to react because he knew he was busted.

I stood up and yelled out to a room full of people doing the test that it was all a fraud, briefly explaining what had just transpired. The Scientology staff was not pleased with my outburst and immediately escorted me out of the building. But following close behind were other people who had been taking the test.

Mission accomplished!

What a deplorable thing to do to someone—tear people down to take advantage of them. Narcissism 101. I currently live close to the Scientology headquarters in Clearwater, Florida, and every time I drive by, I salute them, but not in a polite way.

❧

During 1979 and into early 1980, I did a lot of studio work with a variety of artists. My first recording session was with Greg Lake of Emerson, Lake, and Palmer. I don't think it's necessary to mention that I was a tad nervous—as in sick-to-my-stomach-with-possible-diarrhea nervous. Greg could tell I was a bit out of sorts by the certain shade of fear I wore on my face, so he offered me something that would calm me down.

A line of cocaine.

Yeah, right.

I politely declined the offer, knowing it would cause an immediate aneurysm and complete failure of all bodily functions. The session ended up going well though, and he asked me back to record on a couple more songs. I was pleased with the work I'd done, and so was Greg.

Unfortunately, I found out later that the whole album was scrapped and that he'd started over from scratch. Oh, well, such is the music business, always full of surprises.

I sometimes wonder if cocaine was the result of that decision . . . naw!

8

Ahhh, the Arrival
of the '80s

The '80s were a time of consumerism, materialism, cocaine, fast cars, fast women, endless parties, and complete pandemonium. As well as the "greed is good" mentality of the Yuppies. It was the time of big hair, big shoulder pads, spandex, the dawn of music videos, and MTV. Mix all this together with the ultra-conservatism of Regan Republicans, and you had the recipe that would set this decade in motion. Oh, and what decade it was!

Some of my earliest memories include attending parties in Beverly Hills. Now, these were definitely not your typical suburban backyard barbecue get-togethers. Drugs, alcohol, nudity, fights, debauchery, orgies, overindulgence, and every other form of immorality and lunacy you could possibly imagine were all provided at these sinful shindigs. I didn't necessarily partake in the excessive indulgences, but I was humored as I watched from the sidelines.

Typically, into the third day of these marathons, only a few of the spoiled rich Beverly Hills kids remained. They'd be up the entire time doing designer cocaine in their little social circle, all huddled around the pool complaining about how neglected they were by their parents and how they never had enough money to spend on useless things.

Huh?

They didn't have a clue as to what real-life challenges were about. On occasion, I would psychologically slap them upside the head by educating them on what true hardship entailed. They seemed to appreciate my insight because I was always invited back.

Go figure.

On one such social gathering, the house where the party was being held had formerly belonged to none other than Errol Flynn, the flamboyant swashbuckling movie star of the 1930s and '40s. The new residents knew the history of the house in detail, so I was eager to hear the stories the walls couldn't tell. They shared wild tales involving Errol, W.C. Fields, John Barrymore, Charlie Chaplin, and Clark Gable, as well as numerous others who frequented the historic Hollywood Hills home.

Since the house still held many of its original furnishings, stepping inside felt as though you'd literally traveled back in time to that very era. The dining room had a large round antique table that was purportedly used for all-night poker games and excessive drinking by these iconic celebs. I sat at that very table with the homeowners and a few of their friends that night, enjoying a game of poker with libations. I imagined what it must have been like to sit with those legends of the silver screen and what their conversations may have sounded like.

Oh, to have been a fly on those walls, as the atmosphere in that room was steeped in mysticism.

⚡

At this interval in my journey, I rented a room in a large mansion near the beach in Santa Monica that had once been a hotel Marilyn Monroe frequently used as her beach getaway. She'd hide there to escape the media's prying eyes.

The intense vibe in that mansion was undeniable. Even though it had an elegant setting, sadness seemed to emanate from its walls, something I felt from the moment I moved in. I found out months later that the room I rented had been Marilyn's personal room. The landlady explained that she didn't like to mention it because it might scare prospective clients away.

On the contrary, I felt it a privilege to be so close to her presence.

From Errol Flynn's estate to Marilyn Monroe's beach getaway and all the other iconic places I'd visited during those years, each location shared a history lesson in entertainment legacy, and I absorbed it all. There's an undeniable feeling one gets when in the presence of these legends, even if it's just a place where they once lived. It's both magical and surreal.

While living in Marilyn's beach getaway, vocalist Ralph Mormon (formerly of the Joe Perry Project) and his wife rented another room there. This worked out well, considering Ralph and I had just started playing together in the band Savoy Brown, a group that had been popular during the late '60s and early '70s. The only original member was blues-based guitarist Kim Simmonds. The band also consisted of the legendary bassist Tim Bogert (of Cactus, Vanilla Fudge, and Beck, Bogert & Appice fame) and Keith Boyce, a popular London performer and session drummer. Ralph rode with me to rehearsal since he and his wife didn't own a car at the time. I don't think Ralph could have driven anyway, since he was fairly inebriated most of the time. Bless his heart.

Our first gig took place at the Los Angeles Bicentennial Celebration. Good ol' Ralph was so drunk he couldn't remember the lyrics, so we had to cut the show short. And that's when Ralph decided to introduce the mayor of LA, Tom Bradly.

As the mayor approached the stage to give his bicentennial speech for the city of LA, Ralph blurted out in an obnoxious voice, "Please welcome *fucking* Tom Bradly to the stage, everyone. Get your ass up here, Tom!"

When I gazed out upon the silent crowd, I didn't see one mouth that wasn't hanging open. We probably weren't going to get an invite to come back to play the following year, and perhaps we'd be spending the night in the LA County jail.

Immediately after the gig, Tim Bogert quit the band. I had no idea what the future held, as this project no longer seemed to be walking on stable legs. To make matters worse, our manager told me that while performing any future shows, I needed to stand back by the amps and just play rhythm, with no solos, because they were a bit too complex and flashy for the band's style of music. This didn't go over well with me, especially since I was asked to join the band *because* of my playing style.

Facing those demands, I wanted out of the band straight away. But there was a problem: my contract. Thankfully, the management and I eventually came to an agreement, and I was let out of the contract. In the end, I was disappointed the project didn't pan out, but my philosophy is that things happen for a reason. In my mind, it's always sunny, but I bring an umbrella just in case.

During this time, I met a beautiful and intelligent lady at a party in Hollywood. I can't use her name for reasons that will become obvious later. We struck up a conversation and hit it off right away, and after that night, we started dating regularly. I later learned she was a former *Cosmopolitan* model, which made perfect sense with her striking features and elegant poise. She lived in a beautiful home in North Hollywood and drove two high-end luxury cars. I didn't have a clue as to what she did to make this kind of money, and she always avoided the topic during our conversations. I decided to just enjoy the extravagant lifestyle we shared without being insistent about discussing her profession.

One evening, when we returned to her place after dinner, she opened her purse and pulled out a couple of stacks of $100 bills. This definitely got my attention. She then opened her closet, pulled out a shoe box that was almost full of $100 bills, and placed the new ones inside. While the closet door was open, I noticed several more shoe boxes stacked on the shelves and floor. I asked if they were full of the same content, and she answered without hesitation that they were.

I became a bit concerned, as that's a large amount of cash for someone to hide in their closet. She said it was all just part of her business, and she didn't like using banks, which, of course, sounded very suspicious.

As time went on, she began to disappear, sometimes for days at a time. When I inquired as to her whereabouts, her explanation was always vague and evasive. Everything seemed to be so secretive. It felt like I was living in a mystery, as if my life were being written into a Raymond Chandler novel and Phillip Marlowe was about to walk through the door with a revolver at any given moment. But she assured me it was all legitimate, so I shrugged it off and we didn't discuss it again.

She came to see me unexpectedly one night at my place in Santa Monica. As soon as she arrived, she broke down in tears, pleading with me to leave town immediately. I tried to calm her down and asked what it was all about. She shakily replied that they found out about us and were coming after me.

"Who are they?" I asked.

She confessed she belonged to an organization that demanded she never become involved with anyone. She explained that it could compromise the organization's secrecy, and they made people disappear if they felt they were a threat.

I knew immediately this was not a game, and my life was in serious jeopardy.

She continued sobbing and apologizing profusely. It was sad because, in spite of her strange circumstances, we really had a great connection.

Regretfully, that night, we said our final goodbyes. I grabbed my guitars and some clothes, along with a few belongings, and fled.

I never returned to that mansion by the sea with the comfy little room, the very one Marilyn used to enjoy so much, and I never saw the mystery girl ever again.

↯

As I was hiding from the mob in a shady Hollywood hotel, I came across an ad for a room to rent in Glendale, a small town northeast of LA. I figured it would be far from danger and provide me with a fresh start. When I drove out to meet the guy renting the room, his roommate was in the process of moving out. He looked strangely familiar. When we looked at each other face to face, we burst out laughing and gave each other a big hug.

It was Steve Isham, the keyboard player I knew from the band Big Horn in Seattle.

I hadn't seen Steve since a Fourth of July bicentennial party at my place in 1976. Now, think about this: what are the odds of running into someone you knew years ago who is now moving out of an apartment you're moving into 1,200 miles away from home . . . in a city of sixteen million?

Slim to none!

It was just a few years later when Steve Isham, or Ish, as we called him, would become the keyboardist for the band (Autograph) that would change both our lives significantly.

↯

Making the move to Glendale turned out to be a good choice, for a while anyway. My new roommate, Geary, and I got along great. We quickly became good friends. He was a solid bassist and good songwriter. As a result, we ended up writing songs and playing in a couple of projects together. But things took a drastic turn when Mr. C came knocking on the door.

That's right. The dreaded monster: cocaine.

Our place became party central, with people coming and going 24/7. Snorting marathons lasted for days, we guzzled enough booze to appease the soccer fans of Manchester United, and we endured enough "saving the world" scenarios and doomsday prophecies to make

Nostradamus' ears perk up.

Now, I know I stated earlier that my experimenting with drugs was over, but in the early '80s in LA, it was extremely difficult to have a social life without a bit of indulgence. Once again, I resented allowing myself to be led back into the deplorable lifestyle of drug use. But fortunately, after a year of exposure to this destructive behavior, I'd had enough. I was so desperate to get away from it all that I just up and moved into my car, a 1974 Ford LTD. My new address was:

Steve Lynch

Ford LTD Blvd.

Somewhere L.A., California 90001 (90002, 90003 . . .)

Months later, I'd saved enough money from doing studio work to get my own apartment in Van Nuys, located just north of Hollywood in the San Fernando Valley. This was a welcome change, as it was very difficult to practice guitar in my car, even though it was the size of a small land barge. I used to call it my "Land-bargini."

In my new apartment, I started teaching private lessons and quickly developed a fairly large roster of students. I also began to socialize again (after losing a year in the cocaine academy) by going to various events, concerts, and clubs to get my name out there and make new business connections.

At that time, a friend's girlfriend, who happened to be a Playboy Playmate, introduced me to her friend, who was also a Playmate. Life wasn't sucking at this point. She and I had a lot of fun together, but it was a somewhat short-lived rendezvous.

One night, as I waited for her outside her apartment for a dinner date, a stretch limo pulled up directly in front of me. She got out, followed by a familiar looking character. It was Dan Aykroyd of *Saturday Night Live* and *Ghostbusters* fame. I just laughed it off because she and I weren't seriously involved anyway. I then decided to meet up with some friends at my favorite haunt, the Rainbow Bar and Grill.

Now, for those of you who are not privy to the Rainbow, it's a one-of-a-kind rock club in West Hollywood on Sunset Strip, one the who's who in the music industry frequent. It was also a great place for local LA musicians to meet, do business, and socialize. Most of the bands who formed in the '80s LA scene had a connection to the Rainbow. Had it not been for this famous landmark, many of them would never have come into existence.

If you happen to be wondering, the answer is yes; a lot of drug use, overindulgence, sexual activities, drunken antics, decadence, promiscuity, perversion, and immorality occurred there on a nightly basis. But they also served really good food.

The VIP room upstairs was reserved for most of the debauchery and became like a second home to me.

While living in LA during the early '80s, I played with a variety of bands: Looker, Wolfgang, Viva Beat, Arkenstone, The Word, and Holly Penfield. We played all the popular venues such as the Starwood, Gazzarri's, the Whisky a GoGo, Filthy McNasty's, and the Troubadour. Some of the musicians from these bands would later become members in a new project that was forming, a group that would later gain quite a bit of notoriety.

9

The Birth of Autograph and the Van Halen Tour

Many people don't realize that Autograph didn't just come out of nowhere and form a band. All of us had played in different projects together but formed the actual band later. Keyboardist Steve Isham and I were playing with Holly Penfield on Dreamland Records, singer Steve Plunkett was playing in Silver Condor on Colombia Records, drummer Keni Richards was playing in The Coup on A&M Records, and bassist Randy Rand was playing with Lita Ford on Mercury Records.

In the pre-Autograph days of 1983, Plunk, Randy, Ish, Keni, and I would get together on weekends to drink beer and jam at Victory Studios in North Hollywood. None of us really took it seriously because we all had paid gigs already.

While enjoying one of our beer-soaked jams, producer Andy Johns came down to have a listen. For those who are unfamiliar, Andy was a well-known engineer and producer who had worked alongside his famous brother, Glyn Johns, with numerous big-name bands and artists. Their collective accolades include working with the Rolling Stones, The Who, the Beatles, Led Zeppelin, the Eagles, and Eric Clapton, to name a few. So, obviously, Andy had been around the block a few times. To us, it was an honor to just have him sit in on our little impromptu jam.

We performed a few cover songs for him. Andy was very pleased with our musicianship and overall sound. However, he was more interested in our original material, so we played a few songs we'd written together, including a new song we'd just finished called "Turn Up the Radio."

Andy absolutely loved our originals and asked if we'd like to go into the studio to record a demo. Without hesitation, we all said, "YES!"

As it turned out, Andy was owed recording time at Gower Studios in Hollywood, so the session wouldn't cost us a dime. Perfect for our budget.

The following weekend, we recorded a five-song demo. It took one day to record the songs, and another day—the next day—to mix and master. We were all seasoned studio pros from all the previous recording sessions we'd been involved in, so this was basically a walk in the park.

As it turned out, Andy was very pleased with how smoothly everything went and how well the finished product came out. So, the next course of action came quite naturally and out of absolute necessity: we got spankin' drunk!

What else could we do? There were no other options.

\

Now, this is when the dominoes started falling into place along the Yellow Brick Road. Our drummer, Keni, had a morning routine where he would meet with his pal, David Lee Roth, at 8:30 a.m. to jog up Sunset Boulevard. David, being the lead singer for Van Halen, made it top priority to stay in shape so he could perform his onstage acrobatics. And since Keni and he were friends, Dave invited him along for his morning workouts. This is how the Van Halen/Autograph tour initially came about.

A few days after completing our demo, Dave asked Keni what he was doing musically. Keni replied that he was still playing with The Coup but had just finished a demo with a side project that didn't have a name. Dave asked to hear the new demo, and Keni was more than happy to oblige.

Dave absolutely loved the songs and asked who the musicians were. He had apparently heard of me already and thought it was cool when he learned I was involved.

But when Keni mentioned Steve Plunkett and Randy Rand, his eyes widened. "Wow! Really?"

You see, there's a history between Steve, Randy, and Van Halen, because Van Halen used to open for Steve and Randy's band, Wolfgang, back in the mid-'70s LA club scene. Dave probably thought that everything comes full circle, and it would be cool to have Steve and Randy open for them for a change. So he asked Keni if we would be interested in the opening slot for Van Halen's "1984" tour, starting in a few months.

I think Keni may have soiled himself a little at that moment.

❦

Later that day at rehearsal, Keni popped the question. "Hey guys, Dave asked if we would be interested in opening for them on their "1984" tour. What do ya' think?"

We all stood dumbfounded for a second, then responded with a big: "DUH!" It was like we were part of the cast in *Wayne's World*. The only problem? We were all contracted to other bands. This was rather quickly resolved, though. We all said, "Fuck-em!" A response to be expected from true rockers when an opportunity like this arises.

Next on the agenda: write more songs, book more rehearsal time, raise money, find a way to get to the opening show in Jacksonville, Florida, and come up with a name for the band. No problem. What's a little pressure?

So, we wrote a few more songs, played a private show for donations, rented a Winnebago, and off we went on our merry way. But we still didn't have a name. *That's okay*, I thought, *we'll think of one on the way there.*

So, there we were, making a 2,400-mile trek across the continental US from LA, California to Jacksonville, Florida, in a dilapidated old

Winnebago with no brakes or shocks. But we couldn't have been happier. This was the stuff books were written about. (Hmmm, not a bad idea).

A few days later, as we drove at 25 mph through a windstorm in the arid region of West Texas, I was reminded of an old song and began singing it with a little twist in the lyrics. "Been through the desert in a band with no name."

The rest of the guys joined in, improvising lyrics to fit our situation. This humorous little interlude made us realize it was time to seriously consider what we were going to name the band. We began this process with each member writing down five names on individual slips of paper. We then passed the papers around in a circle, with each of us crossing out the names we didn't like.

One name wasn't crossed off: Autograph. It seemed fitting because we had a signature sound, unlike most of the other bands around at the time. We tended to have more of a '70s style with an '80s twist. So, as we traveled across Interstate 10 in a barely salvageable Winnebago that was riding on only two wheels due to the fierce windstorm, we all concurred. Autograph it is.

Now pass the whiskey, dammit!

ϟ

We arrived in Jacksonville, Florida, on January 18, 1984. It was my twenty-ninth birthday, and we were ready to hit the stage to a sold-out crowd of 18,000. To say we were a bit nervous would be a gross understatement. Then, while I was practicing in the backstage hallway right before we were to go onstage, I was visited by Van Halen's tour manager.

"Are you Steve Lynch?" he asked.

"Yes," I replied.

"Are you the one who wrote the book about the technique of using both hands on the guitar neck?"

"Yes."

"You are forbidden to use that technique on the tour because it's Eddies' thing," he said harshly.

That didn't go over well with me, not in the least. I informed him the material for the book was written in 1978 while I was attending the Guitar Institute of Technology, well before I'd ever heard of Eddie. "Am I allowed to use a pick or is that Eddie's thing too?" I asked sarcastically.

"If I see your right hand on the neck one time, you'll not only be fired from the tour, but you may need to find another profession other than playing guitar."

Two muscle-inflated goons stood beside him, glaring at me as if they'd enjoy nothing more than to rip me apart like vicious pit bulls at their master's request.

I decided it best to relent. It looked like the tour wouldn't be the fun-filled, exciting adventure I had been anticipating. And I didn't want anything to do with it. The threats and scare tactics were straight out of a mafioso playbook, and I didn't like the method of intimidation nor the rules.

After this little altercation, I went into our dressing room and explained to the band what had just transpired. They reacted with disbelief and didn't understand what the big deal was with me playing my own technique. At that point, I had no desire to play, but I wasn't about to throw away the opportunity of a lifetime.

All things taken into consideration, we took the stage and proceeded to kick ass. I managed to get through the songs by improvising my solo parts rather than playing the two-handed ones I'd written, so all went well. I later found out the orders to inhibit my playing didn't come from Eddie; it was just the management worrying about how it might upset him.

But Eddie didn't seem concerned about it, and it didn't matter anyway. A few weeks into the tour, as I was backstage after the show getting a bit lit on Jack Daniels, Eddie walked by. Being slightly inebriated himself, he came into the dressing room where we began to chat it up. I showed him my book, *The Right Touch*, which he was already familiar with. We proceeded to exchange a few licks and talked about our birthdays being so close together, mine on January 18, 1955, and him on January 26 of the same year. Being the same age with similar influences, we got along well.

I explained to him what had happened on the first night when their management informed me I wasn't allowed to play this technique because it was "his" thing. Eddie said he had known of me for some time from hearing my name being mentioned in relation to the two-handed technique, but explained he was unaware of the incident. He said he didn't care what I played onstage, encouraging me to play whatever I liked. This was music to my ears, as I had tremendous respect for him and didn't want there to be any weird vibes, which, between the two of us, never existed anyway. From that point on, I played my solos as I'd written them, Eddie and I got along great, and the dogs were held at bay. I found their management was polite and accommodating after that. They were just looking out for their best interest, which I understood completely. All was good in the world of rock and roll.

↯

While on tour, an unexpected but welcome thing began to occur after our performance each night. We were receiving offers to sign a record deal from a variety of labels, including Geffen, Warner, A&M, Atlantic, Capitol, Epic, and RCA. This was something none of us expected. In the beginning, we had only planned to go out for a short time to play a few shows and then head back to LA to our regular gigs. However, temptation was knocking hard, and we were answering the door. We talked among ourselves about the potential repercussions if we were to break our contracts, then weighed that against having our own record deal with a band we loved playing in together. On top of that, we were getting a *ton* of exposure from this tour. For an unknown band, this was huge.

Literally backstage on tour, we negotiated with record companies to decide which was going to be the best fit. At Madison Square Garden in New York City, we came to an agreement with RCA. They knew there were a lot of competing labels vying for our signatures, so, to offset the competition, they offered us 100 percent of our publishing rights to seal the deal. Now, anyone in the recording industry knows that's unheard of. Record labels always take 50 percent of publishing rights off the top. It's standard for new deals. So there we were, signing a three-album recording contract with RCA backstage at Madison Square Garden.

Yes, indeed, the dominoes were definitely falling in the right direction.

꘡

Being on a tour such as Van Halen's "1984" came with a few good stories. Almost every night, bassist Michael Anthony walked off stage after their show and directly into our dressing room, wearing his Jack Daniels bass and carrying a full bottle of Jack. He'd always keep that Jack Daniels bass on until the bottle of Jack was finished. This was his modus operandi. Occasionally Eddie, Alex, and Dave would pop into our dressing room to get away from the madding crowd (the media) and party with us as well. They always received a warm welcome. We hung out as good friends and, of course, we partied like rock stars.

꘡

One night, after a show at the Omni in Atlanta, Dave came back to our dressing room and bellowed out, "Let's go to a strip club!" We overwhelmingly agreed to accompany him and embarked on this much-desired excursion. Dave insisted that, instead of taking limos to the club, we travel via the new subway system called MARTA (Metropolitan Atlanta Rapid Transit Authority). So, Dave, the five of us, Van Halen's management, and four security guards all hopped on MARTA and away we went. Poor MARTA, she was never quite the same after that.

Upon arriving at the Cheetah Lounge gentleman's club, we stormed in like an invading army of '80s hair and attitude. The club's security staff sat us next to the stage by conjoining a few tables into one row. While there, a comedian got on stage to release a few dirty jokes, which were not that funny, considering we were living testaments to those jokes. Soon after starting his routine, his attention took aim at our table, particularly at Dave. The guy didn't have a clue who he was and began making fun of Dave's appearance and demeanor.

Bad idea!

After a few jabs back and forth between the two, the comedian invited Dave on stage to have a little battle of wits, so to speak. Another bad idea. You see, Dave was very witty and had years of experience dealing with hecklers, so he wasn't about to give in to this guy's verbal crucifixion without a good fight. What happened next was sheer hilarity. Both Dave and the comedian threw vicious barbs at one another for ten minutes straight. The whole audience was in tears from laughing so hard. In the end, the comedian gave up and collapsed on his back onstage. Dave promptly placed his foot on top of him and raised his hands in triumph. That earned him a standing ovation.

Bravo!

A short time into the tour, we'd earned enough to trade in our Winnebago for a real tour bus. Well, let's just say it had more wheels than the Winnebago, otherwise it wasn't much of an improvement. This thing was on its last legs—or wheels, one might say. The bus came equipped with a tall, lanky driver named Bat, who'd seen better days as well. He was often mistaken for a meth addict and, for all we knew, he may well have been. We traveled many a mile in that tattered old bus and were just happy to have transportation and heat, especially after the Winnebago's heater had gone out in the middle of winter in the upper Midwest—not a good time or place to be without heat.

At one point while playing in Detroit, the temperature fell to an icy -62° with wind chill, freezing the bus's fuel line. Now, we're talking brutally cold. Us LA boys were not used to this arctic lifestyle in the least. Bat came up with a brilliant idea to thaw out the fuel line by using a blow torch. For some reason, this didn't sound safe to us—fire and gas? But we were hungry, cold, tired, and didn't want to deal with it, so we wandered off to our hotel rooms, leaving Bat to his little Evel Knievel experiment.

The next morning, when we tried to open our hotel room doors, they wouldn't budge. They were completely frozen to the door jam from the outside because the wind had blown snow and ice into the seams. We called the front desk to rescue us, but they were unable to do anything. So, the manager of the hotel had to call the fire department to thaw the ice from the doors.

When we were finally set free, we found Bat under the bus still trying to thaw the fuel lines. The first thing he said was, "Ain't gonna work, boys. 'Fraid yer gonna have ta fly to da next gig."

So there we were, sitting in the hotel lobby, waiting for a couple of taxis to bring us to the airport, all of us deathly ill from the flu and uncertain if we could find flights to Cleveland for our show that night.

Luckily, with the perseverance of our tour manager, we found flights, made it to the show, and hit the stage right on time. I'm still not sure how we pulled these things off.

After the frozen bus incident, Bat wasn't looking much like a healthy rodent, so we thought it best to replace him. He agreed. He was sick, tired, completely fried, and just wanted to go home (to his cave). For a replacement, we hired his brother, Wingnut, to finish the tour. Yes, you heard it right, Bat and Wingnut. (You can't make this stuff up.) Wingnut was a giant step sideways. He was very much like his brother, with the same tweaked-out look and lanky stature, often mistaken for a meth addict. He only lasted for a few weeks because he turned out to be as crispy as his brother, if not more so.

We made the decision to let him go one evening while at a truck-stop diner. He sat across from us at a table by himself, just fiddling with two forks he'd intertwined. He continued this warped little routine the entire time we ate, silently sitting there with bloodshot eyes, playing with the forks as if on the brink of a scientific breakthrough.

This all happened around the same time RCA requested we leave the tour and come back to LA to record our debut album. It made perfect sense. After all, we were out there busting our butts on the road with no product to promote. So, after we let Wingnut go back to his cave to hang upside-down alongside his brother, we went home to start recording.

The "1984" tour with Van Halen undoubtedly lived up to our expectations of what a *real* tour was all about. We were very grateful to the band and will always be indebted to them. Had it not been for them, none of this would've been possible.

Despite all the misbehaving and over-indulgences along the way, we learned a lot. Any musician who's been on tour for long stints at a time will attest to the fact that touring is *not* what most people think. It's a lot of work. But once you've earned your proverbial road legs, you find the journey is well worth the effort.

10

Turn It Up!

The boys are back in town! And we are pumped to get into the studio and get things rolling. Literally, as in "rolling tape."

Once we got back to LA, we went to RCA headquarters on Sunset Boulevard in Hollywood to sign the final documents and seal the record deal. After which, the vice president of RCA opened his desk drawer and presented a mirror heaped with a small mountain of cocaine accompanied by five rolled-up hundred-dollar bills.

Now, there is something I must explain: if you didn't do cocaine in Hollywood during the '80s, you were considered an outcast, not part of the "in-crowd." You were thought of as a goody-two-shoes or, worse yet, a narc. Being sober would make people very suspicious, and, as a result, you weren't trusted. Most would think people *doing* drugs are the ones not to be trusted, but not in LA.

I loved LA in the '80s.

After the signing and everyone had snorted enough nose coffee to complete a triathlon, the band jumped in a limo with the vice-prez and headed out to our favorite hang, The Rainbow Bar and Grill. The celebration went from 3:00 p.m. that afternoon to 3:00 a.m. the next morning. I got home at about 4:00 a.m. and, as soon as I walked in, I heard the phone ringing.

Very odd for that time in the morning. I picked it up and said, "Hello?"

"Is this Steve Lynch?"

"Yes."

"It's Paul Stanley from KISS calling."

"Yeah, right!" I replied and hung up the phone.

Immediately, the phone rang again. Same voice.

"It really is Paul from KISS," the voice said quickly. "I got your number from Mike Varney at *Guitar Player Magazine.*"

At that point, I thought he might be telling the truth. I'd been featured in Mike Varney's "Spotlight" column in the January 1983 issue and had spoken to Mike on the phone several times since. So, it was reasonable to assume he was legit.

When Paul explained that Mike Varney had sent him a copy of the demo I'd sent to Mike the previous year, it all started to make sense. I apologized to Paul for hanging up because I thought someone was playing a joke. At that, we both laughed. After this little misunderstanding was cleared up, he didn't waste any time and got right to the point.

"I've listened to your guitar demo and played it for the rest of the guys, and we're considering you as our new guitarist," he said.

I was deeply flattered and let him know it right away but had to explain my recent RCA deal. He understood and was very gracious about it, saying he wished us all the best. I thought that was considerably generous and wished him luck in their search for a new guitarist. In this business, just like any other, sometimes the timing isn't quite right.

But, as I stated before, things happen for a reason.

⚡

Once we had fully recovered from the Van Halen tour, we found ourselves crossing the threshold into one of the most prestigious studios in the world, the Record Plant. The icing on the cake was when we found out RCA had blocked out a full month in the largest and most well-equipped room there, Studio A. For those who are unaware, when time is blocked out in a studio, it means you have total access 24/7 and no one else is allowed in the room during this time. This, in turn, means the settings on the mixing console, any outboard effects, and the amp and mic placement cannot under any circumstance be changed without our knowing. So, each time we went in, everything was just as we'd left it from the previous session. We felt like royalty, but, on the other hand, we were fully aware of the daunting task that lay ahead: making a hit record.

From the very start, everything went smoothly. We loved working with our British producer, Neil Kernon, who's worked with the likes of Elton John, David Bowie, Thin Lizzy, Yes, Judas Priest, Queensryche, Dokken, Supertramp, and Queen, to name a few. Neil was on the same page with us every step of the way, which made the sessions run both effectively and efficiently. Since all of us were seasoned pros and quite familiar with working in professional studios, we were able to record our parts quickly. This, in turn, allowed room for additional creativity and experimentation.

We recorded the basics—the drums, bass, and rhythm guitar—within five days. After that, Steve Plunkett laid down his final rhythm guitar parts, followed by Steve Isham's keyboard parts. Then it was my turn. Neil Kernon, Steve Plunkett, and engineer Eddie DeLena were in the studio while I recorded my rhythm parts. However, when I recorded my lead parts, I didn't allow anyone in the studio except our engineer, and he was only there to push the record, rewind, and stop buttons.

I make it a point to be well-prepared for the studio and know exactly what I'm going to play on each song. So, to me, anyone who isn't necessary in the room is a distraction, and I rely on complete solitude to focus on capturing the best performance. I always record my parts in the control room, where the recording console and engineer are. This allows me to hear exactly what it's going to sound like when it goes to tape. Yes, I said "tape." Everything back then was recorded analog (directly to magnetic tape) rather than digitally (audio waveform sampled in numeric value).

With no interruptions or distractions, I was able to record and double all my rhythm and lead parts in three days.

When I "doubled" my parts (recording the same part on another channel), I always recorded the first track with the tape running at 99 percent, slightly below normal speed. This means when the tape is played back at regular speed, the pitch is slightly higher than normal. On the second, or "doubled" track, I recorded with the tape speed at 101 percent so that when the tape is played back at regular speed, my guitar is slightly below pitch. This technique, I found, gave a fuller, more unique texture and made my guitar slightly out of pitch, which I prefer.

The next step was to record the vocals. Since Steve Plunkett, Randy Rand, and Steve Isham were all singers, this went rather quickly. Steve Plunkett belted out the best performances I'd ever heard him do, and within a few days, the harmony vocals were completed as well. With all parts recorded, we now had time to analyze what we'd put together. We listened to the songs again and again, discovering parts that could be added, parts that needed a better performance or pitch correction, the length of the ending fade, and any necessary tempo changes.

Some songs felt like they dragged a little. Others felt too fast. This can be corrected by speeding up or slowing down the tape speed. The only drawback is that when you do this while recording on tape, it changes the pitch of the song slightly, as noted previously. Musicians who later try to figure out the songs by ear in standard pitch become confused and frustrated. I imagine them asking, "What the hell tuning are these guys in?"

When the mixing (adjusting the volume levels, equalization or EQ, and effects on each instrument) was completed, we each took a cassette copy to listen to in our cars and home stereo systems. The next day, we'd share our opinions and tweak things to make the songs satisfactory.

Once we finished the mixing, we sat in the studio and listened to the final product. At that moment, we knew we had something special. Neil Kernon did an outstanding job, and the performances from each member were brilliant. All in only thirty days! I was incredibly proud of what we'd accomplished. It was exhilarating! That recording was a major pivoting point from being a musician with a dream, to living that dream. It was surreal. To this day, any time I listen to what we created back then, I get emotional. It's a special feeling that never quite goes away.

Upon completion of our debut album, *Sign in Please*, we were swept into the old Charlie Chaplin Studio to film the video for our first single, "Turn Up the Radio." Now, here is an odd twist to the story: RCA thought the song "Send Her to Me" was more commercially feasible for radio than "Turn Up the Radio," which we thought was insane.

Hello? The words are literally, "*TURN UP THE RADIO!*" a title that may suggest radio stations would like it.

After debating with RCA to even record the song—they were initially opposed to it—we were now disputing whether it should be the first release. Fortunately, our video director, Ollie Sassoon; manager, Suzy Frank; Paul Atkinson from RCA; and the band; all thought the first video should be for "Turn Up the Radio." In the end, we won the argument.

To put this into perspective, everything would have turned out entirely different for us if RCA had gotten their way. I can't imagine the alternative. As it turned out, we did film a second video for "Send Her to Me." But it didn't receive nearly the recognition as "Turn Up the Radio." So, we were right in the end.

Brilliantly, RCA struck a deal with Paper Mate pens to pay $125,000 for the video production, so long as we were seen holding the pen in the video intro. We agreed. Why wouldn't we? Otherwise, we would have had to pay for the video out of pocket, which would have been taken out of our mechanical royalties from the album sales.

Most people are unaware that record companies don't usually pay for any of the costs in recording fees, promotional material, video expenses, marketing, equipment, touring, and so on. They will invest the money upfront, but the artist must pay it ALL back before they see one dime from record sales. This means you must sell a "lot" of albums before you're able to eat and pay the rent.

What came next were two exhausting, sixteen-hour days of filming. Filming a "keeper" required several takes of each scene to get the correct lighting, sound levels, synchronization, and camera angles. After filming all the scenes and completing the editing, we had a finished, MTV-ready product. But it had one setback: MTV didn't allow commercial props in submitted videos, which meant they wanted the Paper Mate scenes to be edited out. Big whoops! Lucky for us, they agreed to air the video without any editing since the scenes with the pen were relatively short. The video went into heavy rotation for several weeks, which, in turn, boosted radio play, which meant more record sales, which resulted in more *cha-ching*!

11

Takin' a Bite of the Apple

O ur next adventure took us to NYC. *Ahhh*, the Big Apple! While there, we attended the New York Music Expo at Madison Square Garden where I'd won the Guitar Player of the Year award. I'd been so busy touring, recording, and filming videos that I forgot I'd submitted my guitar demo to the Music Expo Committee the previous year. So, I was completely taken off guard when I won.

After receiving the award, I was informed I would sit on a panel with other guitarists to perform a solo and then participate in a Q&A session. Little did I know, the panel consisted of jazz and blues guitar giants Al DiMeola, Les Paul, Johnny Winter, and Larry Coryell. When I walked up on stage and sat down, I thought for sure I was going to throw up on them. When I stood up to perform, my hands literally shook as though I was having a seizure—at Madison Square Garden, nonetheless! And to make things worse, when I looked down into the audience, standing right in front of me was the wizard of two-handed jazz tapping, Stanley Jordan. I desperately wanted to slip into an alternate dimension. It was just too much.

But to my own amazement, I stood up there and proceeded to play my ass off for five minutes straight, which was the longest I'd ever held my breath. After I finished performing and regained my senses, I realized where I was and almost passed out. To my even greater amazement, the audience and panel applauded enthusiastically and cheered me on.

Backstage after the event was over, I talked with the guitar greats from the panel for a few minutes. They were curious about the two-handed technique and, to my surprise, began asking questions about it. As I explained the theory involved, Autograph's manager, Suzy Frank, came walking by with copies of my book about the technique, *The Right Touch*. So, I gave them each a copy and brief instructions on how to read my method of writing and how to play it.

At the end of the evening, after a few jokes and some hugs, we all parted ways. Never in my life would I have imagined being in the presence of these icons, let alone perform in front of them. While I was leaving, the evening rose to its crescendo when I noticed Les Paul in a little room backstage, sitting on a chair, holding his guitar with my book on his lap and his right hand tapping away on the guitar neck.

"I see you're stealing my guitar licks!" I blurted out.

"And I'm not giving them back!" he responded.

We both had a good laugh about that little interlude.

I thought, *Wow! It just doesn't get any better than this!*

✱

The other purpose for our visit to New York was to meet all the corporate big-wigs and staff at RCA headquarters. It was a great privilege to meet the president, Bob Summers, and discuss RCA's marketing strategies for Autograph. Later that evening, the band and several RCA personnel went out to dinner. We ate and drank like kings and partied throughout the night.

When we arrived back in LA, our management received a bill from RCA for $10,000. We had no idea what it was for. Our manager,

Suzy, called them to figure it out. They told her it was the bill from the restaurant we dined at in NYC.

Remember when I said the record company doesn't pay for anything? Case in point. Although they invited us to dinner, *we* were the ones who ended up paying the tab. Thank you very much, RCA. Next time you want to take *us* out for dinner, it's going to be McDonalds.

12

Walk This Way:
The Aerosmith Tour

When we went on tour with Aerosmith, we had to tone down our typical on-tour antics. No alcohol or drugs were allowed backstage or on our tour bus. We also had to stay at hotels located on the opposite side of the city from where Aerosmith stayed. Their management was adamant that we work under these conditions while touring with them. They explained that promoters were very hesitant to work with Aerosmith because they had canceled shows in the past due to drug use, and a cancellation could bankrupt a promoter.

Now, you may think this doesn't sound much like a rock and roll tour, but there was ample reason for these rules and regulations. You see, Steven Tyler and Joe Perry had just gone through a tough bout in rehab, so there was to be NO temptation whatsoever from us. It didn't bother us at all. We wanted to support their sobriety in any way possible, as we felt privileged to be touring with such a legendary band.

But even before we went on stage for the first show of the tour, Joe Perry walked up to me and asked, "Steve, do you have a bump?"

For those of you who don't know what a bump is, it's an inhalation of a small bit of cocaine up your nasal cavity. The effects are as follows: your sinuses feel like you have just shoved a Q-tip soaked in red-hot Tabasco sauce up your nose, your heart rate skyrockets into near cardiac arrest, you immediately confess your life story to anyone within hearing range, and your bowels let you know something is brewing downstairs. Cocaine is not recommended as a laxative, or for those with sinus problems, a heart condition, or who have things they don't want to confess.

I apologetically informed Joe about the restrictions their management put on us, and that we would be fired from the tour if any of us were to grant his wish.

Steven Tyler's case was slightly different: he was fighting his heroin addiction as if his life depended on it, which it did. One night, after the show, as Steven and I were having a discussion, the topic of heroin addiction came up. I confessed that I'd gone through a bout with it when I was fifteen and that after being strapped to a bed with a shower curtain beneath me for three days, I survived the withdrawals and never dared touch it again. He was intrigued by the story and amazed that I didn't have any desire whatsoever to revisit the dreadful "Mr. H."

He then said something that really stuck with me: "Heroin is the last thing on my mind before I fall asleep at night and the first thing I think of when I wake up every morning."

I saw him thirteen years later on a talk show saying the exact same thing. It saddened me to hear that after all those years, he was still fighting it. I'm so grateful both Steven and Joe were able to kill that dreaded beast. Because of this, they were able to continue being the brilliant musicians they are and kicked ass for decades to come. Bravo guys!

⚡

We'd just finished playing a show in Providence, Rhode Island when a strung-out looking hippie chick just walked on our tour bus as if she were part of our entourage. Each of us thought one of the others must have invited her, or that management had arranged an interview with her, which was often the case. We started talking with her, but she didn't seem to make any sense and wasn't able to explain who invited her onboard, or what she was even doing there. We began to realize she was either tweaked on drugs or just plain psycho. Or perhaps a bit of both.

Then we noticed a pungent odor permeating the atmosphere, and believe me, it reeked. At this juncture, our bus driver, Mojo, was pulling onto the freeway.

Suddenly, out of nowhere, he turned his head around and blurted, "What the fuck is that smell!?"

In response, we all pointed at the hippie chick as she continued rambling on, making no sense whatsoever.

Mojo immediately pulled off to the side of the freeway. "Get the fuck off my bus!" he yelled.

She became very agitated, but exited the bus as requested while ranting that we were a bunch of assholes. As we drove away, watching her on the side of the freeway in the heavy snowfall, she held up her two middle fingers and screamed, "Fuck you, Aerosmith."

We simultaneously broke into hysterical laughter that lasted all the way to our next destination. She thought she was on Aerosmith's tour bus. You really can't make this stuff up!

❧

A few days later, we found ourselves in San Antonio, Texas, recording a live album for the King Biscuit Flour Hour, which is broadcast live nationally. After playing a near-perfect set, the band had to rush to the airport to catch a flight to LA so we could perform on *American Bandstand* the following morning. As we exited the backstage door, we saw something none of us expected: a blizzard. In San Antonio. This was unheard of! The band crammed into taxis and rushed off to the airport while the crew and bus stayed behind to prepare for the grueling drive from San Antonio to Detroit. As we approached the airport, we noticed blockades had been put up to cut off incoming traffic. The airport had been shut down due to the unexpected weather. We drove around the blockades to make it to the airport anyway. Even though our flights had been canceled, we had to try our hardest to make it to LA on the first available flight the next morning.

There we were, stuck in an abandoned airport with no food or anything to drink other than the water from the airport water fountain. Yum! Then something miraculous happened. Chris, our tour manager, whipped out a big bottle of vodka from his suitcase. Hail King Chris! As we passed the bottle around, Chris pulled out two red Solo cups and duct-taped them together at the rims to create a reasonable facsimile of a football. We then formed teams and proceeded to play solo-cup football and drink vodka in the abandoned airport while a freak blizzard roared outside. This is what musicians call "improvising."

By morning, the storm had passed, the airport reopened, and we were able to catch a 6:00 a.m. flight to LA. Once we arrived, we raced to Dick Clark Studios to prepare for filming. We had to get this done fast because we had a flight to Detroit leaving at 2:00 p.m. to play a show that night. We found Dick and his wife, Kari, to be the most gracious hosts imaginable. They knew we were crunched for time, so they did everything possible to make sure our filming segment happened promptly. Dick became frustrated when the boy singing/dancing group performing before us couldn't get their dance steps synced to the music. He kept running up to our dressing room to let us know they should be ready for us any minute. About twenty minutes later, he burst into our dressing room with his face flustered and bellowed: "If those *fucking* little brats don't get their shit together, I'm going to kick them off the stage." Then he slammed the door and ran back down the stairs.

Hearing this, we all looked at each other. "Did Dick Clark just say the F-word? How cool!"

In the end, we made it through filming and back to the airport just in time for our flight. Definitely *not* something I would have gambled on. From doing a live album one night to getting stranded at the airport that same night, making it to LA to film a song on *American Bandstand* the next morning, and flying to Detroit that afternoon to perform a show that night, I think we did pretty damn good and deserved a rest.

But a rest didn't happen. We had to do an interview and photo shoot after the show and then go out to dinner with the venue promoter at a restaurant in Detroit's Greek Town. And as it turned out, Bob Seger was there celebrating his birthday with Jamie Lee Curtis and Aldo Nova, as well as a host of others. When Bob saw us, he invited us to join the celebration. We figured it would be the gentlemanly thing to do, so we granted his request.

Unfortunately, after ingesting enough ouzo to puke licorice, we had to drive to Cleveland that night to play a show the next night. By the time we arrived it was early afternoon. We couldn't wait to get to our hotel rooms to get some much needed sleep . . . but not so fast. There was a television interview scheduled, which we were in no shape to do. As a result, we never did get any sleep. We had to go to the venue for soundcheck and then perform.

After such a whirlwind over the past few days we didn't even know where we were, so when our singer Steve Plunkett went up to the microphone and belted out "How ya doin' Cincinnati?" it didn't go over well with the audience, considering we were in Cleveland. Now, try doing this for a year straight, and we'll gladly greet you at the gates to the asylum.

As soon as the tour with Aerosmith ended, we went back to LA and right into the studio to record our second album, *That's the Stuff*. Once again, we found ourselves back at our home away from home, the Record Plant. As before, RCA blocked out Studio A (our favorite room) for a full month. But we didn't have a producer. Regrettably, Neil Kernon, our previous producer, was recording with another project, and we didn't have the time to wait for him to finish due to our tight schedule. We contacted Andy Johns, who'd produced our first demo, but he was busy with another project as well. So, RCA recommended a producer for us, and, after listening to his work, we thought he'd be a good fit.

❧

Since we'd written most of the material for this album while on tour without having the luxury of making demos first, there were some necessary rewrites and tweaks to do as far as song arrangement and specific vocal and instrumental parts. This process went quickly since we were all on the same page ideologically.

After working with our chosen producer for a few days, we realized he didn't have much input regarding production ideas and thought perhaps he didn't like what we were doing. But when we spoke to him about it, he reassured us this was not the case. He told us that watching us work was like observing a well-organized musical beehive. That everything we did was done efficiently and with an overabundance of ideas, so he didn't feel the need to chime in. He just enjoyed watching us work.

After discussing the matter in more detail, he and the band decided it best to part ways and that we self-produce the album with our engineer, Eddie DeLena. We didn't tell RCA we weren't working with the producer any longer, so whenever one of the personnel from RCA stopped in to check on our progress and inquired as to his whereabouts, we'd respond by saying he went back to his hotel for a nap, or was getting something to eat. Of course, we eventually had to tell them we sent him home, which didn't go over very well. They didn't like the fact that we avoided telling them. But they certainly liked the way the album was sounding. And that's all that really mattered anyway.

Upon completing the recording, it was time to film the videos for the singles. The songs chosen were "That's the Stuff" and "Blondes in Black Cars." While filming "Blondes," the director decided to film my solo section out in the desert with a few beautiful blondes. I thought this was a great idea. We only had one trailer to use as a dressing room, so between takes, the models and I had to cram into this little tin can like sardines. It gave me something terribly difficult to deal with. I had to be in the trailer while all these gorgeous models were doing their costume changes, which meant I was alone in this confined area with a plethora of gorgeous naked women.

I sat there thinking, *Now, this is what I signed up for!*

When I informed the band about the harrowing experience I had to endure, they all yelled at me, flipped me off, and tossed their drinks on me.

I just sat there and smiled.

13

From Brian Adams to Ronnie James Dio to Heart

You wouldn't expect a band like Autograph to go from touring with radio-friendly Brian Adams straight into a stint with heavy-metal singer Ronnie James Dio and then another one with the melodic rock band Heart, but that's exactly what we did.

As soon as the album and videos were completed, we were back on the road. Brian was an amazing performer, and his band was exceptionally tight. On our last show in Norman, Oklahoma, a cattle auction took place during the day at the venue we were scheduled to play that night. They had to clear out the cows and then rake the arena with a tractor before we could perform.

Unfortunately, it didn't get rid of the manure smell. Instead, it seemed to enhance it. And when we took the stage that night, the audience was standing smack dab in the middle of the stench, which didn't seem to bother them at all. Being from farmland, they may have become accustomed to it. But being from LA, we most certainly weren't. There were cattle in LA, but they were of a different breed, often referred to as "The Hollywood Herd," or, more simply put, the locals.

On that last night of the tour, as we began to play "Turn Up the Radio," Brian got up on stage with us to sing along. The audience loved it! And toward the end of his set, he looked over and saw us standing by the side of the stage and thought it would be cool to get us up there with him. So, between songs, he had his crew brought up extra mics for us to sing through. We got onstage and sang "Cuts Like a Knife" along with him. And, of course, we all knew the lyrics.

For those of you who have never seen Brian perform live, I must inform you, he spits a "lot" while he's singing. When he came over to our mics during the chorus sections, he drenched us in saliva. The audience was laughing because they could see us getting sprayed every time he came over to sing and could see us wiping our faces as soon as he turned away. When Brian realized what was happening, he started laughing as well, which made us all break out laughing to the point we could barely finish the song.

When it was over, Brian joked to the audience: "Now that Autograph is freshly showered, we bid them farewell and wish them happy journeys ahead."

The audience thought this was hilarious.

We then thanked Brian and the other band members for a fantastic tour and scurried off to our next show the following night with Ronnie James Dio.

We went from one end of the musical spectrum to the other in twenty-four hours. I was amazed we didn't suffer some form of musical whiplash.

❧

After driving all night, we arrived at our next destination early the next morning. We checked into our hotel to sleep for a few hours before soundcheck. When we got to soundcheck, Ronnie welcomed us onto the tour with a big smile and open arms. We'd just seen him before we went out with Brian Adams at Mates Rehearsal Studios in North Hollywood, but this was different. We were now touring together.

This tour was significantly different from the one with Brian Adams, as one might surmise. The audience for Brian was mainly hot young women, sometimes bringing their significant others to tag along. The audience for Ronnie was the exact opposite. It was 90 percent headbanging stoner dudes in black T-shirts who occasionally brought their significant others to bang heads together in unison. One audience had a mush pit, the other had a mosh pit. Go figure.

On one occasion, Steve Isham, our keyboardist, and I were walking backstage after the show when I noticed the little door to the room where they pushed the racks of chairs. The door was only about four feet high. Ronnie is only about 5' 4" (with heels).

I pointed at the tiny door. "Ish, that must be Ronnie's dressing room entrance."

Immediately after saying this, I heard laughter bellow out behind us. It was Ronnie. I thought, *Oh shit!* I told Ronnie how sorry I was and that it was a very insensitive joke.

"No, Lynch, that was good. You really made me laugh," Ronnie said. He told me the timing couldn't have been better with him being only twenty feet behind us. After that, he invited us to his real dressing room for a drink.

"Oh, wow. This door is of regular height," I said while entering, like the smart ass I am.

Ronnie immediately turned around and punched me in the shoulder, which made us all break out in laughter.

Ronnie was such a great sport throughout the tour. Not only was he incredibly talented, but he was also a genuinely nice guy. He passed away in 2010. We miss him very much, and always will. Thanks for the memories, my friend.

↯

Our next tour took us out with the Seattle-based band Heart, whom I'd met on a few occasions in the early '70s, being a Seattle-based musician myself. It was like a homecoming for me to see them again after all those years. Heart was such a great band, and we felt it a privilege to watch them put on such incredible performances each night. Ann's voice was always perfect. I never heard it crack once, even with all the torment she put it through.

Autograph realized that Ann and Nancy Wilson could out-party ANY of us. We were no match. And what made it even more fun was Nancy's then fiancé, movie director Cameron Crowe, was always hanging out filming us onstage, backstage, and on our tour bus. He documented it all. I would love to see some of that footage, Cameron. (Hint, hint.)

❧

Now, if you think touring with Brian Adams, Dio, and then Heart would be a bit bizarre, you are correct. Looking out into the audience while touring with each of these bands was like teleporting to alternate realities. From the innocent, lovelorn fans of Brian Adams to the demon-worshipping headbanging black T-shirt mammals of Dio to the date-night emotional fans of the Heart audience, Autograph seemed to move through a multiverse. At the end of these three wildly diverse tours, we didn't know whether to love the audience, kill them, or just puke.

14

There Is Lunacy . . .
Then There Is Mötley Crüe

It was the tour of all tours. Mötley Crüe and the "Theater of Pain." We survived this tour. Barely. It was like looking into a kaleidoscope of perversion, debauchery, immorality, degeneracy, self-indulgence, and profanity, with an overabundance of sex, drugs, and rock and roll mixed. Yes, we were on the fast track to dystopia. But at the onset of this tour, I also understood that I might have to take a slight detour from the madness afterward. I knew beforehand what I was in for.

On the way to the first show, our equipment truck slid off the road and flipped over, damaging most of our equipment. Luckily, none of our three crew members inside the truck were injured. I thought of this incident as an indication of how this tour would unfold. I was right. The rest of the tour was one calamity after the next.

It was awesome!

One of our first stops was New Orleans. This is where the party really got started. The members of Autograph and Mötley Crüe went to the French Quarter and indulged in drinks called Hurricanes (the name perfectly describes the effect). They were mixed with every type of alcoholic ingredient imaginable, and possibly some hidden ingredients as well.

After three Hurricanes, Keni was belly dancing for sailors, as a joke of course . . . I think? Later into the night, we stumbled into a place called The Dungeon. The place looked like a depository for bikers, drug dealers, prostitutes, strippers, occultists, cons, ex-cons, hedonists, swamp dwellers, and every other earthbound reptilian imaginable. We fit in perfectly. Our mission there was to find "blow," a.k.a. cocaine, for the uninitiated. It was mandatory our mission be successful so we could achieve a boost, thus granting us the ability to drink more alcohol.

Upon entering, we asked a few bikers if they knew where we could score. These tattooed oak trees replied by sneering, snarling, and spitting on the floor. I was beginning to think making it out of there alive should be our main objective. But in the end, we completed the task at hand and headed back to the tour buses, which transported us to our next adventure—or misadventure, depending on your perspective.

⚡

While touring with the Crüe, Autograph played extra shows on the side. We usually played eleven days in a row and then took one off to recoup. On one such sideshow, we booked a gig at a county fair in the Deep South. As we drove our truck and bus down a long, bumpy dirt road and approached the site of the fair, we became confused. There was no stage—none that we could see anyway. We asked the grounds personnel where it was, and they pointed to a flatbed truck.

No friggin' way! I thought.

To make this work, our crew had to assemble a downsized version of our stage gear so it would fit. To our dismay, the venue didn't supply a dressing room. As if we really thought they would anyway. So, we had to put on our rock and roll outfits and make-up in the tour bus.

When we walked onstage (the flatbed truck), we entered into what appeared to be a distorted otherworldly realm. Silence fell over the grounds. Complete silence. Like, not even a bird chirping. The audience looked at us as though we were a carnival freak show. We peered back with our mouths agape in shock. There was nothing right about what we were seeing.

As I gazed out into the audience, I couldn't see one eye that was the same height as the other, nor one ear that stuck out the same as another. Teeth must surely have been considered a luxury item, and every head of hair looked as though it had been trimmed with the same set of sheep shears. Now, I would never purposely make fun of anyone with "unique features," that's not my nature, but this was far beyond anything I'd ever experienced.

Some people were so cockeyed they could look at me on one side of the stage and Randy on the other simultaneously, without moving their head. A few in attendance were unusually large. Now we're talking "fork-lift-required" type of large. I am by no means disrespecting or intentionally demeaning anyone of sizable physique, it's just that I've never seen a female Jabba the Hutt (except maybe on the TLC channel). I thought all of this might be perpetuated by intentional design, or perhaps "accidental" inbreeding. Who knows? "Mah sista is mah mama, mah brudah is mah uncal, and mah dahta is mah cosin." (Try to figure that last one out.)

We were so freaked out by what seemed like a bad acid trip that we only made it through three songs before bidding the hillbilly natives farewell and making a hasty retreat to the bus. Still, there was nothing. Only silence. As we were leaving, I kept hearing the theme from *The Twilight Zone* over and over in my head. I could've sworn I saw Rod Serling off to the side narrating the epilogue in black and white while smoking a cigarette.

We escaped the distorted-reality fairgrounds pretty much unscathed (at least physically) and found our getaway down a backwoods country road, as silent as the audience we had just left behind. Then, as if on cue, we busted out laughing! Did we *really* just experience that? Tears streamed down our faces, smudging our eyeliner as we passed a bottle of Jack around, barely able to catch our breath long enough to take a swig.

About forty minutes into this backwoods drive, Mojo, our bus driver, told us he had to make a stop for coffee and cigarettes. Once we were parked, he vehemently demanded we not get off the bus for *any* reason. Out of curiosity, I peeked out the window, only to see a dilapidated cabin at the back of a gravel parking lot surrounded by old, beat-up, rusted pickup trucks. At that moment, Randy and I realized we were almost out of cigarettes. So, being a tad bit intoxicated, we decided to ignore Mojo's cautionary warning and enter the forbidden zone to make our purchase. The second we walked through the cabin door, I knew we'd made a huge mistake.

The interior of this "lavish" establishment was dimly lit, but I could make out a dirt floor with wood shavings strewn about. The stench was horrid, like they were probably stewing up some roadkill in the back. Then, the unthinkable happened. While standing there with smeared eyeliner and dressed like a Liberace duet, one of the redneck hillbilly patrons noticed Randy and me.

"Well, Yee-haw! Looky what da cat done dragged in," he yelped.

Every redneck hillbilly in the place turned to ogle us as if we were their drag-queen dates. Mojo stood at the opposite end of the bar by the cigarette machine, and when he turned around and saw us, he came rushing toward us yelling, "RUN! RUN!"

Randy and I saw the panic in his face, so we didn't hesitate to bail as quickly as possible, making a mad dash for the bus. Mojo was right behind us, followed by a dozen ravaging toothless characters similar to those in our previous audience.

Just before jumping on the bus, one of them hollered, "Damn. Come back here, boy! Yer purdier den mah wife!"

Randy and I were now stricken with panic. Mojo hurled himself into the driver's seat, shut the door, thrust it into gear, and gunned the accelerator as beer bottles broke against the side of the bus. He was hyperventilating and his face was beet red, probably the result of being

extremely irate and scared to death simultaneously. He blurted out
a barrage of profanities at Randy and me that would shame a Hell's
Angels grandmother.

After traveling down the road for about a half hour, Mojo, still looking
in his side-view mirrors to see if we were being followed, explained what
the consequences of not listening to him could have been. He told us
most people from these parts don't follow rules or regulations and that
they're pretty much unaffected by the law since the local sheriff and
deputies were usually in on whatever laws they chose to disobey.

"Remember the movie *Deliverance*?" he asked.

"Yes," we chorused.

"Well, that's the kind of picnic they would've taken you on. You'd
all be screaming like little piggies, then prepped by granny for the
evening BBQ."

As if on que I picked up my guitar and started playing the *Deliverance*
theme. Even Mojo laughed at that.

❧

We played a few more shows with Mötley Crüe in the south and then
made our way back toward San Antonio. But before heading out from
Jackson, Mississippi, we stopped at a Chinese restaurant Mojo had raved
about. After our gracious host seated us, our Chinese waiter came up
to the table.

"Well, howdy, boys. How ya'll doin' ta-nite?" he belted out in a
heavy southern accent.

We were in disbelief. This did not compute. We thought perhaps
Mojo had set this up as a joke. But no, this was the way this man actually
talked. We inquired about his accent.

"I's bawn 'n rayzed in deeze pawts, like mah papa en mah papa's
papa bafor hym," He replied.

We all just sat and observed. We couldn't quite grasp the dialect
coming from his frontal orifice. A hillbilly redneck trapped in a small Asian
man's body. We'd never encountered this species before. To counteract

the effect and get our mental equilibrium back, we decided to order our food with a Chinese accent. Billy, the waiter/owner, absolutely loved this. Now you had rock and rollers in drag ordering from a Chinese menu with Mandarin accents and a hillbilly Asian dude with a heavy southern accent taking our order in a feng shui diner in Jackson, Mississippi. It just doesn't get any better!

After finishing dinner, Billy joined us for a few beverages. We laughed and joked around for the next two hours, right up until Mojo told us it was time to hit the road.

One thing you never fall short of on tour is the variety of characters you meet along the way. It makes for some great memories and stories.

As we drove away, I opened my fortune cookie. To my surprise, it read, *You Will Have Diarrhea in One Hour.*

❧

Our next show in San Antonio went brilliantly, and the audience was especially receptive. Following our performance, we met a gentleman backstage who happened to own a strip club nearby. He invited us to stop by for drinks—on the house. So, living up to our reputation as choir boy rejects, we jumped on the bus, drove to the strip club, and proceeded to sin it up. As the night lingered on, a bevy of strippers flocked to our table, trying to coax us into the back rooms (which, in actuality, are little classrooms where they educate you about carnal knowledge). Yeah, right.

One stripper didn't quite fit into one gender. His/her name was Sam, and being from San Antonio, we dubbed her "Sam Antonio." She later told us she was a transsexual, which made sense considering the obvious presence of an Adam's apple, muscular physique, husky voice, masculine jaw, and boob implants with a small patch of whiskers between them.

One band member became a tad infatuated with Sam. I'm not going to tell you which member, but it wasn't one whose first name was Steve. Now remember, there were three Steve's in the band, so the culprit had to be either Keni or Randy. Hmmm, let's see, drummer or bass player? Could've been either. Anyway, Sam was invited on the bus by that "person of interest" and traveled with us for a couple of weeks. She was liked by everyone and became kind of a fixture with the band and crew. She made sandwiches and mixed drinks, ran errands, did laundry, cleaned up the bus, and helped with catering backstage. We really enjoyed her company. It was like always having a mom/dad around.

Rock and Roll. Ya gotta love it.

Not long into Autograph's touring history we became known as the "Party Ninjas." Our fans gave us this nickname because we partied with them *every* time we came to town. And this nickname became our mantra nationwide. In fact, some of our fans made a wall plaque engraved with this title for us to hang backstage when the after-show carnival began each night

❧

While touring with Mötley Crüe, we occasionally ended up on each other's tour bus. It didn't really matter because we were all going to the same destination anyway. On one such occasion, I was on the Mötley Crüe bus drinking a *lot* of Jack Daniels with Tommy Lee Mötley Crüe's drummer. The bathroom on their bus was on the opposite side from the bathroom on ours, and being a bit shit-faced, this confused the hell out of me. I ended up peeing in their closet, ruining their sound engineer's new pair of sneakers. He wasn't very happy about it, but I compensated him enough by purchasing two new pairs. He stopped growling at me after that.

When Tommy and I woke up the next afternoon, we were both so hungover that even our hair and teeth were hurting.

The first thing Tommy said was, "Dude, I don't know how the *fuck* I'm going to play tonight."

I had to agree; I felt the same.

While performing our set that night, I had to run behind my amps twice to puke, but somehow, I kept playing. I still don't know how I pulled that off. Backstage after our set, I found Tommy sitting on the floor in the hallway. He didn't look well at all, as in fifty shades of pale.

He looked up at me. "Dude, what did we do to ourselves last night? I don't know how I'm even gonna get on stage"

And by the looks of him, I didn't know how he was either.

I thought it best to keep an eye on Tommy during their set, especially since I'd puked twice while playing our set. He was doing fine up until his drum solo. On this particular tour, the drum riser would hydraulically elevate several feet during Tommy's solo and then glide out over the audience, turning upside down as he played.

About halfway through his solo, he started projectile vomiting all over the audience. At first, they cheered, thinking it was part of the show. But it wasn't long before they realized Tommy was actually throwing up on them. After emptying the contents of his stomach, Tommy resumed playing his solo while the audience below screamed at him for saturating them with bile.

What a trooper! I thought.

A few shows later, when playing the Omni Arena in Atlanta, Tommy got a surprise visit from his then-girlfriend, Heather Locklear. She was a real sweetheart and would hang out with us whenever Mötley Crüe played their set. One night, she excitedly rushed into our dressing room and said, "I just asked Tommy to marry me, and he said YES!"

As we congratulated her and exchanged big hugs, Tommy walked into the room.

"Dudes," he said. "You've got to come to the wedding."

There's no way we were about to miss this! So, we gladly accepted the invite.

The wedding ceremony was held in Santa Barbara at a private estate with park-like grounds. It was an exquisitely elegant event, especially by rock and roll standards. Every who's who from the Hollywood scene was present. Famous actors and musicians, managers, producers, directors, agents, and every LA band you could think of were in attendance. The parking lot looked like an exotic car exhibit, and there were enough stretch limos to transport the entire population of Guam to the event.

The ceremony and reception went without a hitch, that is, until Tommy decided it was time to step up the party a notch or two. Champagne and shots of every kind of hard liquor imaginable were distributed like a production line while cocaine was passed about like nasal Pez dispensers.

It was fun to sit back and watch all these Hollywood celebs indulging in their sinful delights as if no one was watching. It was the perfect rock and roll wedding.

＼

While on stage during the Mötlies tour, gazing out into the ocean of breasts in the audience, an idea came to me. *Hmmm. I wonder, if I put a sign on the back of my guitar that said, "SHOW ME YOUR TITS!" and lifted it while performing for all to see, would they follow the directions?*

So, later that night, I took white duct tape and spelled it out on the back of my black guitar. When finished, I showed the band my creation. They all thought it was a fantastic idea. Then, we came up with another idea. We could have Billy and Crease (two of our stage crew) run out and put backstage passes on whoever revealed their boobies.

It worked like a dream! I ran from one side of the stage to the other, lifting my guitar to show the sign. And—WHAM! Up would come the shirts and out would come their lovelies. It turned into a masquerade onstage. Plunkett would point out a girl in the audience, and I'd run over and lift my guitar. Then Randy, Keni, and Ish started pointing out willing participants.

By the time our set was over, we had enough airbags backstage to equip a fleet of Toyotas.[5] Our dressing room was like one of those huge blow-up attractions at Chuck E. Cheese, the one kids bounce around in—except ours was for adults.

---

5   Now mind you, this story is in no way intended to offend or disrespect anyone. That's the last thing I'd want. Its intent is for humor only.

A month later, the tour brought us to the Pacific Northwest, my home. The show was held at the Tacoma Dome, a 23,000-seat auditorium in the city of Tacoma, just south of Seattle. This show marked the first time my family would see me play live. My mom and dad, brother and sisters, and nieces and nephews were in attendance, along with all the dear friends I'd grown up with. This was an epic time in my life. This was the very moment I'd worked for since I first picked up the instrument, and I was wrought with anxiety. It was my proving ground. I had to show my dad that I'd followed my dream, and that it had paid off.

When the lights went out in the sold-out arena, the crowd roared. I thought, *Fuck it. I'm going to play my ass off!* And I did. In fact, I never played better. Autograph took the stage and owned it.

I peered out to see where my parents were and spotted Dad first. It was easy to spot him because he was the only bald head in the mosh pit. I smiled and pointed to him, and he smiled back, as he was being tossed about as if in a blender of malevolent souls. Next, I spotted Mom and knew not to expose the back of my guitar with its *wording* for fear she might reciprocate. (Just kidding, Mom!) She's in heaven now, laughing, and probably saying, "Steven, shame on you!" just as she did every day of my youth.

Seeing my family after the show was the best part. I felt that, in some way, I'd brought them all together again. It seemed that even though we may have drifted apart, we were still only an arm's reach away in our hearts. To have everyone laughing, smiling, and sharing memories of days gone by was more than I could have hoped for. Even now, when I look back to that night, I realize it was the best show I'd ever played, and it always will be.

On our flight back to LA after the tour, I sat next to Mick Mars, Mötley Crüe's guitarist. All the other Mötley Crüe and Autograph lads were on board as well. As expected, the flight was an airborne atrocity. An endless onslaught of one cocktail after another, signing autographs, taking pictures, and snorting cocaine. It was like being backstage, except we were 35,000 feet in the air. There are *no* laws when you're that high (literally). Once we landed at LAX, Mick and I couldn't get our boots back on because our feet had swollen up, which tends to happen during flights when there's an overabundance of alcohol consumption. We had to walk off the plane in our socks, carrying our boots. Everyone laughed, including us. We then parted ways and went home to prepare for the encore event: night golfing in the San Fernando Valley. With the members of Autograph and Mötley in attendance, this was surely NOT going to resemble anything remotely close to a pro tournament. Quite the contrary, I assure you.

The valley has a nine-hole golf course that lights up at night. You use colored fluorescent balls to follow where they go and identify which one is yours by its color. We had our own golf carts and hired four alcohol carts equipped with bikini-clad bartenders to keep the libations flowing. It's LA, what can I say? These things are considered normal.

We rented the entire course for the night, but we had to rent it after midnight, which was fine by us. By our standards, midnight was considered early evening. Accompanying us was an entourage of about thirty people, many of whom had never played golf. It didn't really matter; it was just an excuse to keep partying anyway. A combination of *Caddyshack* and *Animal House* would be the perfect way to describe this sport-less event. And it surely would've earned full approval from both Bill Murray and John Belushi.

15

Loud and Clear

When the aptly named "Theater of Pain" tour with Mötley Crüe was over, I again thought about the way I felt about this lifestyle. My life was not going in the right direction. Although it had been a lot of fun, the outlandish behavior I was participating in was not really me. I noticed a change in the way I perceived things. It was as if the experience had awakened something inside.

It was time to make some adjustments. I decided to go straight. It was time to get back to my roots and focus on what all this was really about: making music and playing guitar. Even though I constantly practiced while on tour, I knew my playing wasn't as good as it could be. I wasn't playing with the precision and conviction I'd once had, and it had a profoundly negative effect on me. I'd lost an integral part of myself due to the excessive partying. It made me realize just how far I'd strayed from my path and how desperately I wanted to get back on it. So, in December of 1986, I quit everything. Drugs and alcohol were out. My mind, body, and soul thanked me emphatically.

I guess you could say my true confession is that, although I love playing guitar and creating music, the rockstar lifestyle never quite fit.

I realized my natural desire was to live a more purposeful and dignified existence. Something better was waiting. And this caused me to re-evaluate what the future might hold.

❧

After two weeks of recouping from the tour, Autograph was back in the Record Plant for our third album, *Loud and Clear*. We had more time to write for this album, and at this point in our careers, our songwriting was at its absolute best. And this time around, we had Andy Johns producing for us. It was exciting to be working with Andy again. As I'd stated before, we wanted to work together previously on our second album, but his schedule wouldn't allow it. Now, both our schedules were open, and we had three months blocked out in Studio A—more than enough time to produce a quality product.

Andy was meticulous in the studio and came equipped with some unique and interesting ideas. On one occasion, he wanted to get a fatter sound on the snare drum. To attain this, he experimented with firearms to get the sound he was searching for (not always a good idea to utilize deadly weapons with an Englishman who drank gin for breakfast). After acquiring the necessary arsenal, we stacked cement bags in a soundproof room at the back of the studio and placed a variety of microphones around the room for an ambient effect. Then the fun started. We fired numerous shots from a selection of guns into the cement bags to record the sounds they produced. The result sounded like an anti-aircraft cannon going off. He then combined this sound with the snare drum so that every time the snare was hit, the cannon would go off. Absolutely brilliant!

Since we weren't pressured for time, some periods had a slight lull in the recording process. During one such time, Andy wanted to liven things up a bit.

"Let me make a phone call, lads," he said.

A half hour later, two strippers showed up.

I wondered, *Hmmm, where's Andy going with this?*

He instructed the exotic dancers to get atop the piano and do their routine. Now, mind you, this was a $500,000 Bösendorfer grand piano, handmade in Germany. It was *not* meant to be used as a stage for stiletto-heeled strippers.

Once the dancers completed their routine, we examined the piano for damages. And sure enough, there were a couple of scratch marks on the black gloss lid. Andy knew he'd have to pay for the repairs out of his own pocket, but he didn't seem to mind because his plan worked: the dancing duet was inspirational and, as a result, we got a lot of work done that night.

Bravo, Andy!

When it came time for me to record my solos, Andy and I had a slight butting of heads. Andy wanted me to play more blues-like instead of incorporating the style that defined me. This didn't go over well with me, as I already had all my solos worked out. So, I politely threw his ass out of the studio until they were completed.

When finished, I played them back for Andy. His response was, "That's fucking brilliant, Lynchy! You followed my instructions perfectly!"

We got a good laugh out of that, both knowing I didn't listen to *any* of his suggestions.

Upon completing the album, we went back to New York for a press release, a photo shoot, and to guest host MTV's Headbangers Ball with Ozzie Osborne.

When Ozzie first arrived with his wife/manager, Sharon, Ozzie had only been out of rehab for two hours and was noticeably uncomfortable filming sober. During this time, Ozzie had a spiky haircut, which stuck out in every direction (with the help of a can of Aqua Net, of course). He was so nervous that his spiky hair shook all about as if he'd stuck his finger in an electrical outlet in the rain.

The director kept saying, "Ozzie, we can't film until your hair stops shaking."

This only made his anxiety worse, and since he had the opening segment, he had to read the teleprompter for the entire introduction. It didn't go well.

"Hello, this is . . . " he began, and that was it.

"Fuck! Roll it again," he blurted.

After about twenty attempts to get through the first sentence, he turned to his wife. "Sharon, go get me a six-pack."

"Ozzie, you've only been out of Betty Ford for a couple of hours," she replied.

So, he tried reading the teleprompter a few more times, but with the same results.

He finally lost his temper. "SHARON, GO GET ME A FUCKING SIX-PACK NOW!"

Sharon must have known the situation wouldn't improve without the help of some liquid courage because she eventually complied and went to get his six-pack.

When she returned, Ozzie popped one bottle after the next downing the whole six-pack within twenty minutes.

"Okay, I'm ready. Let's roll," he said to the director.

This time, he got the whole intro perfect on the first take. Ya gotta love Ozzie.

⚡

After returning to LA from New York, we started the video shoots for our first two singles, "Loud and Clear" and "Dance All Night." We rented the Long Beach Arena, a 13,500-seat venue southwest of LA, for filming both videos. On the first shoot, for the song "Loud and Clear," we decided not to have an audience. This made it appear as though we were doing a soundcheck before the show. We invited Ozzie and Vince Neil (the lead singer from Mötley Crüe) to be in the video—which they were more than glad to be a part of. Thanks, guys!

On the second shoot, for "Dance All Night," we publicly put word out beforehand that we were filming a video so people would have the chance to participate as the audience. We didn't expect the Long Beach Arena to be filled almost to capacity for a video shoot, but it happened. The band was grateful so many people showed up and stayed for the entire shoot, which lasted ten hours. This showed us how truly dedicated our fans were. And rest assured, we let them know how much we appreciated their unwavering devotion by taking pictures with them and signing autographs for hours after filming ended.

As you may recall, I vowed early in my career that I'd never turn down a picture with someone, or fail to give them a guitar pick, or sign an autograph, and I still hold to that standard to this day. Thankfully, my bandmates felt the same. Besides, we *had* to sign autographs; we *were* Autograph!

Before going back on the road, I had to finish writing my second and third instructional manuals—*The Right Touch*, books 2 and 3.

Since I was on such a hectic schedule, I had to finish the books pronto. I completed the writing first and then recorded the tapes accompanying the books. This turned out to be an especially arduous undertaking because I had to do everything in my home studio by myself. That entailed verbally introducing the page and section of the book I was going to demonstrate, recording the piece, and then explaining how to play it step by step. I couldn't make any mistakes while performing any of the three steps because I didn't have an engineer to hit the play, record, and rewind buttons. Recording wasn't fun, and I exercised my right to abuse every profanity imaginable several times over. But I finished by the deadline, and the end product came out much better than expected.

Next, I had to fly to Seattle to film my instructional video *The Two-Handed Guitarist* for REH Videos. I only had one day to film the entire thing, and there was a "lot" of material to cover. Since I flew in a day before the shoot, I had a chance to visit Dad and ended up staying with him while in town. It was a bit awkward at first since I'd only seen him a few times since the age of fifteen (including the concert with the Crüe) and I was then thirty-two. But we bonded rather quickly and realized we had a lot of things in common, especially our sense of humor, which helped the awkwardness dissipate within a matter of moments.

While staying at my dad's, I ventured into a room he renovated after I had moved out seventeen years earlier. What I saw in that room caught me off guard. It was dedicated entirely to me. He had newspaper clippings, gold albums, magazine articles, interviews, awards, photos, and everything else I could imagine neatly framed and hung on the walls. I just stood there and looked around in awe. I had no idea Dad had collected all of this, or that he even cared. I fell to my knees in that room and cried like I had never cried in my life.

This meant *everything* to me. It showed something I'd never realized before, how deeply I cared about how my dad felt about the choice I'd made to become a professional musician. He thought I was never going to succeed, so it was important to me to prove him wrong. All I'd ever wanted was to make him proud. Right then and there, I felt I'd succeeded.

From the day he'd kicked me out of the house at the age of fifteen because I quit school to dedicate my life to guitar, and through all the turbulent times I'd experienced while continuously working toward that goal: living penniless in a tent, playing sleazy bars, practicing relentlessly, constantly traveling, attending the Guitar Institute, living in my car, struggling to survive day to day, in constant turmoil, and desperately clinging to my sanity and my dreams. In the end, it all came down to one thing: I'd made my dad proud. It was all well worth the effort.

The next morning, after that amazing revelation, I was in West Seattle filming my instructional video. And to my surprise, the director was my old guitar teacher, Don Mock. The one who, in 1978, encouraged me to quit my band in Seattle, sell my equipment, and move to Hollywood to attend the Guitar Institute—the decision that changed my life. This was indeed a very nice surprise. Except that when we started filming, I realized I was *still* nervous about playing in front of him because he was my teacher, and so damn good! After all those years, little had changed.

As when I recorded the segments for my books, there was no room for error. Not only did I have to perform everything perfectly, but I also had to narrate it without any mistakes. All in all, the filming went without a hitch, and eight hours later, we had a finished product that everyone was more than satisfied with, including me.

The following day, after saying farewell to my dad, I went to my mom's place to visit with her. My brother John met us there, and together, we had the most enjoyable time catching up, laughing, and reminiscing about our childhoods. Then it came time for me to leave, so we said our goodbyes. I rushed to the airport for my flight back to LA to start my next adventure: filming a live video for a new major motion picture.

Throughout Autograph's travels, we periodically flew back to LA to record songs for movies and television such as *The River Rat,* starring Tommy Lee Jones; *Youngblood,* starring Rob Lowe; *Fright Night,* starring Chris Sarandon and Roddy McDowall; *Secret Admirer,* starring C. Thomas Hall and Kelly Preston; *Miami Vice, Hunter, The Amy Fisher Story,* and the list goes on, including video games. But here we were filming a "live" video for a new movie called *Like Father, Like Son,* starring Dudley Moore and Kirk Cameron.

Yet again, we found ourselves at the Long Beach Arena for the filming. The song chosen for the soundtrack was "She Never Looked that Good for Me" from our album *Loud and Clear.* Working with a major motion-picture production company was quite different from what we were accustomed to. Not to diminish working with a music video director in any way but working with the director and crew of a major motion picture was a different level of professionalism. There was no lag time, and everything was by the clock. These guys were fast, confident, and efficient.

After a few practice takes, the director said, "Let's do one more rehearsal to get the sound levels right."

Since we thought it was just a rehearsal, we didn't take it seriously. We ran around goofing off while playing the song. I spat mouthfuls of water on Keni and he threw drumsticks at me. The rest of the band ran around the stage like sugar-rushed toddlers.

"Cut! That's a take," the director said at the end of the song. That meant it was the final performance and they would use that "take" in the movie.

The band immediately disputed his decision because we thought it was just a rehearsal, so we didn't think we performed our best.

"It's one of the oldest tricks in Hollywood," the director explained. "Tell the actors it's just a rehearsal. This way, they usually give their best performance because they're more relaxed."

He played back the clip they'd just filmed, and he was right. It was perfect.

16

Changes on the Horizon

Here we go again. It's 1987, and we're out on the road, headlining for the first time. Boy, I thought, this tour is going to be quite different from the previous ones because I'm clean!

Even though I *never* drank or did any drugs before going onstage, it still felt odd to be out on the road sober, as opposed to being a Party Ninja. It was going to be interesting to perform each night with a clear head and no hangover. And, as it turned out, it was far better than I could've imagined. I played with precision and confidence and felt more comfortable onstage than I ever had. I loved taking command of the instrument and showing the audience the best I had to offer. What an incredible feeling!

On this tour, we were all over the map: East Coast, West Coast, the north, the south, and everywhere in between. Because it was a summer tour, there were a lot of outdoor festivals. We performed shows with ZZ Top, Whitesnake, Scorpions, Night Ranger, Aerosmith (again), and a long list of others.

I was "straight," but the shenanigans hadn't changed much for the rest of the band. So, the partying continued, as would be expected. It was interesting to watch the carnival from the sidelines, void of any substance in my system to alter my perception, but it felt as though I was no longer part of the band. Which I wasn't, aside from performances. I had become an outlier. As a result, I felt a distance between the band and myself. They felt it, too.

I felt alone, and *was* alone, because I chose to be.

My life had become quite different. I was in a much better place physically, mentally, and spiritually. I had replaced my reckless behavior with practicing four hours a day, exercising, writing songs, eating healthy, getting as much sleep as possible, and reading a lot of books on philosophy, psychology, history, and self-awareness. The band would make fun of me because I'd become such a bookworm. But I didn't mind. I was in my zone and enjoyed being there. It's where I needed to be.

Many people don't realize how incredibly difficult it can be to maintain a relationship when you're a musician. Especially when you're always on tour. My wife and I, whom I'd met while touring early on, only saw each other a few days here and there. As a result, unfortunately, we grew apart. We still loved one another, but it wasn't the same with me gone all the time. The last time I had returned home from touring, I felt as if I didn't know her any longer and sensed she felt the same. I also knew she wanted to start a family, which made things more difficult because I didn't want to have children yet, not when I couldn't be there to watch them grow. That was not my idea of fatherhood. I knew I was going to be gone most of the time and, as it turned out, I was. I toured with Autograph for a few more years, then taught guitar clinics internationally for a few more after that. I wouldn't have seen my wife or kids for at least six years, and I wasn't about to let that happen.

Even though we went our separate ways, things worked out well. She remarried a few years later to a great guy, and they now have two grown boys. I couldn't be happier for her.

Throughout most of my career my relationships were fairly short lived. I was always practicing, writing, recording, or touring, so I wasn't able to commit to a serious long-term relationship. I didn't feel it would've been fair to anyone considering I was always busy or away. So, I thought that part of my life would have to wait. I have to admit, there were times this was very difficult. It was just me and my guitar, and that can become very lonely.

After eight months on tour, we were ready to head back to LA. On the day before we left for home, Steve Isham pulled an all-nighter. We went to his room the next afternoon to wake him up and found him still passed out on his bed with his mouth hanging open, drooling (we've all been there). When the phone rang on the nightstand, sitting next to the hairdryer, we thought we'd let him answer it since it was time for him to get up anyway.

He grabbed the hairdryer and held it to his ear. "Hello" he said. Since he wasn't getting a response, he turned the hairdryer on. We watched in hysterics as he yelled, "HELLO!" into his hairdryer while it blew his hair all about. We decided it would probably be in his best interest to let him sleep it off a while longer.

Once we arrived back in the City of Lost Angels, we took a few days off before our next endeavor, which was hosting a benefit called Find the Children to raise funds to help find missing children. It was held at the Roxy Theater on Sunset Strip in West Hollywood. Everyone in LA wanted to be part of this event because of its worthy cause. Members from Mötley Crüe, KISS, Poison, Ratt, LA Guns, Quiet Riot, Stryper, Bon Jovi, and a host of others wanted to participate. Everywhere you looked backstage, people from various bands were rehearsing together to perform songs.

The audience absolutely loved seeing their favorite musicians mixed together playing cover songs. With so many people trying to get into the event, the city had to shut down traffic on Sunset Boulevard. News helicopters flew overhead and police barricades surrounded the perimeter. It was absolute chaos, but in a good way. The event was a big success. It raised more than twice what was expected, so everyone was exceptionally pleased with the outcome.

I love when celebrities put their egos aside and volunteer their time to become involved in a worthy cause. You'll find that when the armor comes off, there's often a good heart beneath. And there's no shortage of that in the entertainment industry.

At the end of the night, many of the musicians went next door to the world-famous Rainbow Bar and Grill. I don't think the place had ever seen so many stars inside at one time in its history. I stayed until closing time, 4:00 a.m.

As I was leaving, the owner, Mario, approached me. "Steve, stick around for a minute. There's someone I want you to meet."

After waiting a few minutes, he took me to a separate VIP room to meet this mystery person, and there stood Jimmy Page, Led Zeppelin's guitarist. I gaped in disbelief and introduced myself.

"I know who you are, mate," Jimmy said, and made a gesture like he was playing guitar with both hands on the neck.

That really took me by surprise. *Jimmy Page knows who I am!*

We chatted for about twenty minutes before parting ways. It was the perfect ending to an amazing day. I was high on life.

As we all know, life brings many changes, some good, some not so good. And what happened next in the history of Autograph was not good. Steve Isham's addiction to cocaine and alcohol seemed to have gotten the best of him. As we were rehearsing to get back on the road, we found him missing in action most of the time. And when he did show up, it was apparent he'd been up for days.

When someone is heavily under the influence of drugs and alcohol combined, with little or no sleep for days at a time, they tend to go into a dissociative state and have little to nothing creative to offer. The fact that he was living with a coke dealer at the time made it next to impossible to guide him toward a healthier, more productive lifestyle. The band kept trying to help, but unfortunately, his addictions had claimed him. Sadly, we had to let him go. It was at this time I realized how much I was beginning to hate drugs.

Ish's departure was especially difficult for me because I'd known him since the mid-'70s. I considered him one of the most decent human beings I'd ever met, and his musical attributes were second to none. But I must confess, when he was at my bicentennial Fourth of July party in 1976 at my house in Seattle, he was already heavily involved with cocaine, and had been for a while. Autograph decided not to replace Ish. Somehow, it just didn't seem right. So, we continued as a four-piece band.

Another change also occurred at this time. Keni Richards decided he wanted to try something different, so he left Autograph to join a new band called Dirty White Boy. We all wished him well and found a replacement drummer, Eddie Cross, almost immediately. Eddie was a wild man. And him being an excellent drummer with a great attitude brought new fire to the band, something that was much needed after Ish's and Keni's departure. We loved playing with Eddie, and he loved playing with us.

After rehearsing for a couple of weeks, it was time to hit the road again. This time we had a new manager as well. Bill Aucoin. Bill was best known in the music industry for his work with KISS and Billy Idol. He was a well-respected manager, but, boy, could he party! Bill was a real character and flamboyantly gay. Somehow, he had the uncanny ability to find the one gay guy out of the entire audience, every single night! We aptly "coined" his ability as gaydar.

Once we completed the shows on this leg of the tour, we headed home to finish recording demos for a new batch of songs we'd written. These songs were for Epic Records, who we were negotiating a deal with after completing our three albums for RCA. Our writing had taken a slightly different direction with the absence of keyboards and, as a result, we sounded heavier, which seemed appropriate for the changing times.

At this time in rock and roll history, a new, more raw style of rock was rapidly gaining momentum. It was called grunge. The negotiations with Epic fizzled out because the market for '80s rock had pretty much become a thing of the past. Seattle's grunge was in, and LA's hair metal was out. Just like that. There wasn't a record company in the country that'd even consider listening to a demo from an '80s band, no matter how successful they'd been. To a degree, I understood why this happened. Toward the end of the decade, '80s music had become overproduced to a point where it felt homogenized, as if it were written for radio play and sales only. This was a result of the record industry's thirst for the almighty dollar. They wanted every song on the album to be a hit and even brought in outside writers to ensure that outcome. So, in turn, the music lost its identity, feel, emotion, spontaneity, and its freedom. It had become a product of corporate greed.

❧

As I witnessed the inevitable fall from grace of '80s rock, I knew my time in the spotlight was over, at least for now. My time of departure had arrived. I had chased my dream and achieved it. It was during rehearsal in December of 1989 when I called it quits. The others immediately followed suit, as they knew it was over as well. And so, this was the end. The end of Autograph, the end of '80s music, the end of a decade, and the end of an era.

Saddened by this reality, I turned off my amp, put my guitar in its case, and drove home.

17

Network 23

While writing songs with Autograph for the proposed Epic Records deal, I found myself drifting into a new style of writing that was more befitting of who I was personally. I wanted to branch out by experimenting with a variety of sounds to create a multi-layered soundscape. This was the perfect time to record what I felt inside and to express myself emotionally without the pressure of composing only radio-friendly material.

I began to demo my new material to get an idea of the direction I was headed and what the finished product might sound like. While doing this, I auditioned singers at my house. This turned out to be a comedy of errors. Let me explain: LA is a very large circus with a lot of clowns, most of whom have no real talent, only imagined. (I'm not being mean, just realistic.)

The first singer who showed up for the audition was about six-and-a-half-feet tall, dressed in white, high-heeled go-go boots, a mini skirt, a flowered blouse tied in front, false eyelashes, bright blue eye shadow, heavy red blush, pink lipstick, and a blond curly waist-length wig. At first glance, I thought it was Dee Snyder from Twisted Sister. But this guy wasn't even a singer, he just liked dressing up in drag, kinda like Dee. (Just kidding, Dee!)

Next up was a short, fat Mexican man who didn't speak English. He became irate when I didn't want to audition him, and he started cursing at me in Spanish. There was even a homeless guy who showed up with his dog, looking for a place to crash. I felt bad and gave him money for dog food and something to eat for himself. Why was this guy looking in the classifieds for a singer position anyway? How did he even find my place? Or get there?

I didn't understand why these people were showing up on my doorstep. I wrote the ad specifically describing what I was looking for. That didn't seem to matter, though. After all, it was Hollywood, the looney magnet of the universe.

After two months of this onslaught of undesirables, I finally found Jon Lester, a.k.a. Johnny Deluxe. He had a uniquely modern look and a baritone/tenor voice, which was exactly what I was searching for. When he showed me some of his lyrics, they were by far some of the deepest, most profoundly original words I'd ever read. The game was on.

⚡

At this time, I already had a record label that wanted to sign me, Sisapa Records, based out of Columbus, Ohio. The company had a distribution deal with CEMA (a record distribution company formed by Capital and EMI Records out of Manhattan).For those who are unaware, a distribution company promotes and distributes records to various retail outlets. Upon finding Jon, I sealed the deal with Sisapa and flew to Columbus to begin recording.

Since I had written all the instrumental parts, laying down the basic tracks went relatively fast. It helped that I'd previously recorded demos for the songs, as they became the foundation. First were the drum tracks, recorded with drum machines, later to be replaced by actual drummers. Chris Frazier—known for his work with Steve Vai, Whitesnake, and Foreigner—was the main drummer and did a spectacular job! Mike Mangini—who also worked with Steve Vai as well as Dream Theater—came in later to lay down a couple of tracks. He was also outstanding! I felt very fortunate to have these monstrous talents performing on the record.

Next came the rhythm guitar parts, followed by bass guitar, keyboards, and additional percussion. Aside from the drums, I played all the instrumental parts myself. All the writing, arranging, performing, and producing I did myself as well, which were starting to wear on me. But I enjoyed the process, nonetheless.

After finishing my parts, it was time to record the vocals. But something unexpected happened. Something that stopped everything in its tracks, so to speak. Jon, the vocalist I'd recruited, had gone on a drinking binge while I laid down the instrumental parts. He was supposed to be in the studio with me finishing the rest of the lyrics, but it didn't seem to be a high priority for him. When it came time to lay down the first vocal track, it was a no-go. His voice was shot. We tried over and over to get even one usable line, but to no avail. The heavy drinking and smoking had taken their toll.

I told him we'd try again the next day, then drove him back to the apartment I'd rented for him. I asked him to rest up so we could get a fresh start in the morning.

When I knocked on his door the next morning, he didn't answer. Worried, I called the apartment manager to open the door for me. I was appalled at what I saw next. Jon was on the floor, passed out drunk, and the place was completely demolished. The walls were full of holes, the sofa and mattress were cut up, the coffee table and lamps lay in pieces, the blinds were torn down, the refrigerator was overturned, and cigarette burns marred the carpet.

The manager immediately called the police and filed a formal complaint. Luckily, she didn't file charges because I agreed to pay for the damages, which were to the tune of $25,000.

That was it for me. The next day, Jon was on a plane back to LA. And I was back in the studio without a singer.

For the next two days, I frantically called everyone I knew in LA and New York to find a replacement, but no one fit the bill. Then came more bad news. I learned Sisapa Records was filing for bankruptcy and were coming to the studio to seize all recorded material and lock the doors—that night!

This is not going to happen, I thought. After all the money I'd spent and hard work I'd invested, there was no way in hell I was going to give it all up. With the help of the engineers, we packed up my guitars and master tapes and loaded them into their van. They followed me to the airport to drop off my rental car and then dropped me off at my terminal. I thought I was home free, with all my recordings secure. But not so fast. While going through security, they informed me I had to put the masters through the X-ray machine. I vehemently refused because it would erase the recordings from the magnetic tape. I desperately tried to explain this to them, but the security personnel wouldn't budge. I finally had them call the head of security.

Being a musician himself, he understood the dilemma immediately. He knew that the X-ray machine would erase everything. So, he helped security manually go through each box containing the tapes. I then rushed to my gate and made my departing flight just in the nick of time. As I stowed the tapes in the overhead compartment and sat in my seat, I realized that I'd escaped by the skin of my teeth. My first solo album, titled *Network 23*, was going to be finished after all. It was just going to take a little longer than expected.

As the plane left Columbus, I leaned my seat back, let out a big sigh of relief, and smiled. I made it. I was headed back to LA with my recordings safely in tow.

18

International Excursions

When I arrived back in LA, I wanted to go straight into the studio to listen to the tracks I'd cut in Columbus. After listening, I realized there were things I wanted to change, as well as parts I wanted to add. I went into Fox Run Studios and Sound City to complete the instrumental parts.

Since Sisapa Records had filed bankruptcy, the expenses for the recording sessions were now coming out of my own pocket and they added up fast—to the tune of $50,000. (That's over $100K by today's standards.) This sum, combined with the $25,000 I paid in damages to the apartment complex in Columbus, had left me in dire straits financially. I desperately needed more money to finish the album. To get it, I found myself changing my musical direction. I began teaching, like I had in the past. But this time on a *much* larger scale.

I embarked on a guitar tour that took me to twenty countries, teaching 325 clinics. I taught in Europe, South America, Mexico, Canada, Australia, New Zealand, and forty-eight of the fifty United States. Teaching these clinics would earn me the money needed to complete the *Network 23* project, but it also depended on whether I could find a singer.

>

The first place I taught was Europe. In addition to music, I'd been studying philosophy, metaphysics, creative visualization, motivational skills, and the laws of attraction for years. So, I thought perhaps while teaching, it might benefit the attending students if I shared some of this information. I created a 34-page booklet of theory on the two-handed playing technique, and on the last page, I included a list of my top ten books on my other topics of interest.

Toward the end of each clinic, I had an in-depth conversation with the students, explaining the importance of incorporating the principles explained in these books into their song writing and playing as well as their everyday lives. Alongside the music lessons, we had conversations about focus, attitude, dedication, creativity, commitment, time management, philosophy, and overall well-being.

I learned later this was very well received. When I returned to the States, St. Louis Music, who sponsored the clinics, informed me they had boxes filled with mail from the various countries I'd just taught in. I wasn't quite sure what to make of it, so asked them to forward the mail to my address in LA.

When I opened the boxes, I was completely caught off guard. Most of the letters referred to the last page in my booklet about suggested reading material. They raved about how this information had changed their lives and how it had given them a new perspective on what it truly meant to be a musician. To think I'd created a positive effect on the students gave me a feeling of gratitude I'd never experienced before. For the next two days, I sat on my living room floor reading these letters, smiling the entire time.

>

The next place I taught was Mexico. The first clinic took place in Mexico City. The next day, as I prepared to travel to a small town four hours outside of the city, I received some inconvenient news. My driver's vehicle had broken down, so I was going to have to take the bus.

Oh boy, I thought, *I sense another adventure—or misadventure— coming on.*

And sure enough, it did.

As I boarded the bus, the sponsors explained to the driver where I was going. But he looked puzzled. This wasn't a good sign. The only seat available was at the very back with a gaggle of goats and chickens. So, I rode the whole way—what ended up being a five-hour trip—with goats trying to eat my pants and chickens pecking at my big hair and pooping on my shoes. This was truly the rockstar life.

When we finally reached our destination, I was the only passenger left on the bus. The driver said something in Spanish and pointed toward the door, motioning for me to get off. But no one was there to greet me. So there I was, standing on a dirt road in the middle of San Somewhero with my guitar and suitcase, getting covered in dust from the wind with my head bleeding from ravenous pecking chickens, poop covering my shoes, and a hole in my pants from the goats who fancied them.

To top it off, I didn't speak a word of Spanish. Life really doesn't get any better, I felt as though I were in one of those old Clint Eastwood Spaghetti Westerns. The whistling theme from *The Good, the Bad, and the Ugly* played over and over in my head: *DaDee DaDeeDa . . . Da Dee Da.*

The people who were sponsoring the clinic eventually showed up and explained that the bus driver was instructed to drop me off in front of the church where I was teaching the clinic that evening.

In a church? Really? I thought.

That night, I taught my clinic to all the townsfolk, many of whom were elderly and didn't even play an instrument or understand English. Funny thing was most of those in attendance didn't know why I was teaching a guitar clinic in their village church while covered in dust with a bleeding scalp, poopy shoes, holes in my pants, and unable to speak a word of Spanish? I was wondering the same thing myself, and didn't have a clue.

❧

My next excursion brought me to Argentina. I really enjoyed the people and their customs, except that everything always ran about two hours behind schedule. I was supposed to do an interview at 2:00 p.m., which took place at 4:00 p.m. My clinic was supposed to start at 7:00 p.m., though people started showing up at 9:00 p.m. The dinner reservation was scheduled for 11:00 p.m., but we sat down to eat at 1:00 a.m. I just went with the flow and took in the laid-back lifestyle of a culture that doesn't necessarily operate on a clock. Which I thought was nice for a change.

The clinics went amazingly well in Buenos Aires and La Platte. The person sponsoring the clinics was Marcelo Roascio, who I'm still friends with to this day. He did an excellent job setting up the clinics and jams, as well as providing a historical tour of the beautiful city of Buenos Aires. I'd go back in a heartbeat!

But next time, I'll leave my watch at home.

❧

Onto my next rendezvous, Australia and New Zealand. Upon landing in Sydney, I immediately fell in love. What an exceptionally gorgeous city. When the promoter and crew picked me up from the airport, I wanted to take a shot at driving because they drive on the opposite side of the road from the States. They let me drive, but I only made it a few miles. After scaring them and myself half to death from near misses, I realized I was way too jet-lagged to attempt driving, especially in rush-hour traffic.

I was so burned-out from the long flight that I couldn't wait to get to the hotel to shower up and get some sleep. But there was a glitch in that plan. While in flight, I had apparently crossed the international date line. So, as it turned out, it was the next day, which meant I had to teach in a couple of hours.

WHAT?

I don't know why they would book a clinic on the same day as a sixteen-hour flight, knowing I'd be crossing the international dateline, but they did. At least I had enough time to go to the hotel to wash up, though it didn't seem to help my marshmallow brain in the least.

As I was getting cleaned up, I noticed something odd in the bathroom. When I flushed the toilet or ran the sink, the water drained down in the opposite direction. I called the front desk to inquire as to why this was happening.

The lady started laughing. "Silly American, you're south of the equator so the South Pole attracts and causes water to drain in the opposite direction."

Needless to say, I felt pretty stupid. And why hadn't I noticed it when I was in Argentina? I also found that you flip the light switches up to turn them off and down to turn them on. My frazzled mind wasn't adjusting to this very well. I thought perhaps if I hung from the ceiling upside down, maybe everything would go back to normal again.

For the next twenty-five days, I traveled the main hubs of Australia—Sydney, Canberra, Brisbane, Newcastle, Perth, Wyalla, Adelaide, Melbourne, and so on. It was an exhilarating experience, and I loved every bit of it.

During my travels, there was one day that I got to spend some time at a wildlife refuge. It started with purchasing a bag of peanuts at the entrance for the kangaroos. But after entering the wildlife area, I didn't see one kangaroo. The tour guide told me to shake the bag of peanuts. I did, and sure enough, big ears came popping up on the horizon. They'd heard their calling, and within a matter of seconds, I had a battalion of kangaroos hopping toward me. It felt surreal to feed these marsupial critters with their little joeys tucked in their pouches, trying to get into my pockets to find more treats.

Even wallabies and wombats turned out for the occasion. I became popular rather quickly. I was the new refuge refugee, and I had snacks!

My next stop was New Zealand. That island country was a slice of heaven on earth. The diversity of the landscape was captivating. It had everything from a subtropical climate and beaches on the North Island to mountains and fjords on the South Island. It was all stunningly beautiful!

I first arrived in Aukland, a city situated on the North Island. This is where I spent the first night before teaching the next day. The people were most generous and made me feel at home straight away. Their hospitality was unsurpassed. After a great turnout for the clinic in Aukland, we traveled to Rotorua, where I had the pleasurable experience of going for a dip in their famous mineral hot springs, which was so relaxing it made me want to just lie there and doze off forever. I then met and had lunch with some of the Indigenous Maori people, who mesmerized me with stories of their history and culture. Afterward, I went bungee jumping, which I'll probably never do again, since it threw my back out.

Over the next few days, we traveled south to Wellington and Christchurch, both of which had their own charming character. In Wellington, there was a Kiwi Café, their version of our Hard Rock Café, where we had lunch overlooking the bay. Exquisite!

Arriving back in LA from New Zealand, I found myself beyond fatigued. Twenty-six clinics in thirty days between Australia and New Zealand had taken their toll. As soon as I exited the plane, I collapsed on the airport floor. My girlfriend was there and saw me go down, so she ran over and picked me up, got me to the car, and brought me home. For the next two days all I did was eat, drink a lot of water, and sleep.

In the end, I questioned if I'd do it all again. The only answer I could think of was, "Hell, yeah!" Even though it was very fatiguing, I couldn't imagine not doing it. I loved it all.

❧

And now, back to Europe. First stop, Paris. While there, I had a strange experience that changed my preconceived ideology dramatically. It all began while driving to a clinic. As we entered a roundabout, I had a déjà vu moment. I had been to this place before, and I remembered it vividly, even though I'd never been to Paris in my life—not this life anyway.

I had the driver pull over, immediately got out, and approached an old lady who was sweeping off her front porch. I pointed to her place and told her I'd lived there before. The interpreter translated for me, and she began laughing.

"That would be impossible," she said through the translator. "I have lived here my entire life, and my father lived here with his parents before that."

But I couldn't shake the feeling. I remembered everything in detail. I began to prove my point to the elderly lady by describing the apartment.

"Upon entering the front door, there is a staircase leading up to the second floor. Once you reach the top, there's a wall with a small alcove containing a statue of the Virgin Mary."

Her eyes widened.

"If you go to the right, you find the living room, which has a small balcony overlooking a terrace. The kitchen is to the left of the living room."

Then her mouth fell open.

"If you turn to the left at the top of the staircase, you'll find a large bedroom with a bathroom on the right. It has a claw foot tub at the far end, next to a window. A balcony in the bedroom overlooks the same terrace as the living room. Both the living room and bedroom have small chandeliers hanging from the center of each ceiling."

Now she looked frightened and began speaking agitatedly to the interpreter.

"She says everything you have just described is perfectly correct," he told me.

The interpreter and the other two traveling with me had the same dazed look. They were completely baffled. Even though I'd always believed in reincarnation, the encounter left me bewildered. It was personal.

That little episode left me feeling disoriented and lightheaded. Everything seemed surreal, as if I were in a dream. How could this be? How could I possibly have a detailed recollection of a place I'd never been? None of it made sense. I had a very difficult time teaching the clinic after that.

The incident prompted me to dig deeper. As soon as I returned to the States, I bought all the books I could find on reincarnation. What I learned surprised me: my experience was quite common. Many cultures consider it perfectly normal.

I concluded that strange occurrences follow me like a shadow, but the results are always positive, and I always learn something inspirational from them.

❧

Next stop was Italy. I fell in love with Italy immediately! I taught in Florence, Milan, Pisa, Bologna, and Venice. My favorite part was driving to each destination. Along the way, I was able to see the lush countryside with the quaint, picturesque villages nestled between. And while in Pisa, I had to pose for a picture next to the Leaning Tower—while leaning, of course. I think this is customary.

❧

I went to Germany after Italy. When I arrived, my first stop was the city of Frankfurt, where I attended Europe's largest music convention, Musikmesse Frankfurt, in the Exhibition Center Frankfurt. This was 1990, just after the Berlin Wall came down. Busloads of people from formerly communist East Berlin were brought in to experience this amazing exhibition for the first time. I followed them and witnessed how they reacted when they entered the building. Many looked around in awe, while others fell to their knees, overcome with emotion.

Those from what was previously known as East Berlin had been living behind the Berlin Wall under Soviet control, so they had very little knowledge of what was happening in the free world. Therefore, most had never seen anything so spectacular: the bright lights, smiling faces, the vast assortment of instruments, conversations taking place in a variety of languages, a mixture of cultures from around the world, and music echoing from every direction. It was all incredibly overwhelming. These things were foreign to them, many not having an inkling it even existed. And now, after being released from the oppressive rule of communism, they could smell freedom for the first time and enjoy the things the majority of us take for granted.

To bear witness to their experience made me smile, but I also found it deeply emotional. My eyes teared up as I watched their reactions. Some were excited, some were bewildered, some were happy, some seemed confused, and some were distraught as a result of living their lives with so much fear and torment without hope.

From that day forward, I no longer took my freedoms for granted.

After leaving Frankfurt, we visited a historic castle in the village of Marburg, a fifteenth century town where little has changed since those days of yore. The townspeople keep the village as authentic as possible. The cobblestone streets lined with traditional "olde shoppes" and baskets of flowers hanging all about gave me the feeling I'd traveled back in time, when the pace was much slower, and things were far simpler.

As we wound our way through the towns of central and northern Germany, I saw an assortment of centuries-old houses, barns, and stables made of brick and clay with thatch roofs. The beauty was breathtaking.

↯

Eventually, we made it to Holland, where they dropped me off at my hotel in Amsterdam. I was to wait there until the local clinic representatives arrived the following day. After checking in and dropping my luggage off, I decided to go for a walk. I strolled through the streets beside the canals, admiring the ornate architecture and some of the oldest pubs in all of Europe. I visited one pub that was advertised as being from the fourteenth century. While there, I needed to use the restroom, so I asked the proprietor where it was, and he pointed the way.

When I found the entrance, to my surprise, I had to duck my head to make it through the doorway. I thought this was very odd, especially since I'm only five feet eight inches tall, so I inquired about it when

I sat back at the bar. The bartender explained that people were much shorter six hundred years ago. I hadn't known this, but it made me feel tall! I would've been considered a giant among the dwarfs of yesteryear.

My new travel team arrived the following day, and we set out for the first clinic in Amsterdam. The next day, we traveled to Edam and the following day, Rotterdam. It felt as though I were teaching in every *dam* city in the Netherlands. As I traveled south toward Belgium, I saw the Dutch countryside, which had some of the most amazing scenery. Fields of multicolored tulips stretched as far as the eye could see, with windmills dotting the landscape and old stone bridges crossing the canals. I was experiencing the real Holland and was going to make sure I returned. Which I most certainly did.

❧

Next on the list: Belgium. Little did I know that in Belgium, they speak different languages depending on the region you're in. To the north, it's Dutch/Flemish; to the east, it's German; and in the south, it's French. Luckily, I had someone who could translate not only English into these languages, but the musical dialogue as well. And she was only nineteen. How could a nineteen-year-old be so proficient in five languages and well-versed in musical terms also? I was very impressed, to say the least.

After the clinic in Brussels, I met a guitarist named Geert, along with his girlfriend, Kathleen. They were gracious enough to invite me out to a local nightclub called The Viking. There, we drank a kegs-worth of Belgian beer (known to be some of the best in the world) and played foosball till the wee hours of the morning. I'm glad to say we've stayed in touch these past thirty-plus years, as I have with many people I've met in my travels. I find it a blessing to have had the opportunity to meet people from around the world and to have cultivated lifelong friendships. It's one of the things I enjoy most about traveling abroad- the people.

❧

I flew out the next day to the land of enchantment, Scotland. I had two clinics there, one in Glasgow and the other in Edinburgh. While signing posters after the clinic in Edinburgh, I had a rather odd encounter with a local Scot. His accent was so thick I couldn't understand him when he said his name, and I wanted to get it right so I could sign it correctly on the poster.

"It's Rikert, dammit!" he said, getting very angry with me.

I asked him to spell it.

"R-I-C-H-A-R-D!" he blurted in frustration.

"Oh, you mean *Richard*," I said.

With that, everyone started laughing, including me.

❧

Traveling south from Scotland, we entered northern England, where our first stop was the quaint little town of Newcastle. Then, it was on to Manchester, where the Industrial Revolution began, and the railroad was invented. Then we headed west to Wales, where I visited one of the oldest castles in all of Europe just outside of Cardiff. We visited a few other mid-England destinations before we made our way down to London, where I taught my final clinic of the tour before heading back to LA.

❧

All in all, I found these clinic excursions would stay with me for the rest of my life. They gave me a sense of belonging on a global scale. The sights, the sounds, the smells, the flavors, the language, the people—each location had its own unique personality and its own place in this world. It reminded me that I wasn't just an American; I was a human being, sharing this planet with everyone and everything. Because of this experience, I felt my purpose in this life had expanded well beyond what I'd previously imagined. The blinders were off. I could now see the larger scope in its entirety.

We are all connected.

19

Coast to Coast

As I gazed out the airplane window while approaching LA, I noticed how smoggy it was. Looking down on smog after spending three months abroad was disheartening. All the places I'd been recently were naturally pristine and well preserved by the inhabitants. Arriving back in LA with the brown sky, litter strewn about, and congested traffic made me realize something: I no longer wished to be there. I asked my girlfriend if she'd be interested in a change of scenery and a change of pace.

"I'm ready. Let's go!" she replied.

We discussed our options but already knew where we were going to end up. Florida. Clear blue skies, white sandy beaches, warm turquoise water, palm trees, lush greenery. All with no smog or traffic. As if to make our decision easier, the day after I got back to LA, there was an earthquake. For me, that was the final straw.

"Let's get out of here, *now!*" I said at that very moment.

She agreed. And sure enough, two days after the earthquake, we had the moving truck packed with car in tow. We were off!

Now, please don't get me wrong, the fourteen years I lived in LA from 1978 – 1992 were amazing. I learned everything I needed to know about the music and entertainment business and beyond. From attending the Guitar Institute, signing a major record deal with RCA, the professional recording experience, making music videos, living through the entire '80s rock era, and on and on. I LOVED IT ALL! And I wouldn't change this incredible experience for anything. But there are points in one's life when you sense it's time for change, and one such time had come.

We left LA around 2:30 in the afternoon. Approaching the Arizona border, I asked my girlfriend if she could try to find reception on the truck radio. She fiddled around with it for a few minutes until she found a news channel. What we heard next was staggering. It was April 29, 1992, and there were riots breaking out in South Central LA and many other areas around the LA Basin. The verdict in the Rodney King trial had just been announced, exonerating all the police officers involved in his beating.

This was not good. We looked at each other in dismay, realizing we had escaped the mayhem just in the nick of time, but we were also saddened by what was transpiring back at home. Outside of Phoenix, we stopped at a pay phone to call friends and family back in LA. Thankfully, all were safe. Everyone we contacted said they couldn't believe we timed our departure just hours before the verdict was read. We didn't plan it that way, it just happened.

When we arrived at our destination in Fort Lauderdale, we phoned everyone to check in on them again and to let them know we'd made it safely. We asked how they were fairing amid the chaos. Everyone responded that they were okay but wanted to do what we'd just done: leave. That turned out to be problematic. Not a single moving truck was available anywhere.

Seems there were many others who were ready to make their departure as well.

Once we settled in Fort Lauderdale, we found ourselves living in a resort community with a view of the Intercoastal Waterway, a network of canals which flow to the Atlantic Ocean. We were in heaven! Sitting on our balcony with the warm ocean breeze and watching the boats pass by was a far cry from our cramped, overpriced apartment with a parking lot view in the smoggy valley we'd just left, and it was half the cost!

Everything was perfect until about four months later. A little incident called Hurricane Andrew decided to disrupt our little slice of Eden. It was a Category 5, the most powerful category hurricane there is. And it was headed directly toward us. We were in what's called a Red Zone, which means mandatory evacuation. Heeding the warning, we packed up enough clothes for a couple of days and drove north to Daytona Beach, just far enough away to escape the hurricane's wrath. After checking into a hotel, we watched Andrew make landfall live on TV. Oddly, there were no signs of the hurricane in Daytona, which was as calm and clear as could be, while just a few hours south, one of the fiercest storms in US history was devastating everything in its path. We watched the whole event take place, with news reporter Brian Norcross braving nature's fury to bring us the story as it unfolded.

The next morning, we awoke to watch the televised devastation. We couldn't believe what we were seeing. Everything south of Miami lay in complete ruin. As we drove back toward Fort Lauderdale, we witnessed the damage the storm had left behind. Downed power lines, trees, and telephone poles lay strewn across the road. Debris from unidentifiable structures was scattered everywhere. We had to carefully navigate our way through it all while dodging any live power lines to avoid electrocution. It took us six hours to get back to Fort Lauderdale, as opposed to the three it took to reach Daytona.

When we arrived, our power was out and remained so for four days. So, we did what had to be done. We partied! The residents in our complex filled coolers with beer and whatever ice they could find, along with wine and cocktails accompanied by daily barbecues.

All the residents got acquainted rather quickly, and we became close to our downstairs neighbor, Jay, who is still a good friend to this day. Once we got to know Jay, he informed me that he played guitar, and I told him I did as well. He invited me up to his place for a little jam session, which I eagerly accepted. While we were playing, he stopped after a few minutes to watch me play, so I just kept going. When I stopped, I noticed he was just staring at me with a blank expression.

He said, "Holy Shit! I've never seen anyone do anything like that before!" at which I busted out laughing. I told him I was the guitarist from the band Autograph. With this, his face went red. He had no idea I was a professional player and recording artist. Jay and I still get together occasionally for a little impromptu jam, but he usually requires a couple of beers to calm his nerves beforehand.

❧

A few months after the hurricane, my girlfriend and I decided to take a trip down to the Florida Keys. Along the way, we had to pass through the devastation Hurricane Andrew had left behind. We didn't say a word to each other. We just drove through in silence, too shaken to speak.

Our first stop was Key Largo, where there's a place you can swim with dolphins. These dolphins were not in captivity; they would enter the reserve in the morning on their own and were let out at night. The dolphins had become friends with the personnel working there and loved the free fish they received all day for swimming with the visitors.

One of the staff members recommended I swim with a seventy-year-old dolphin named Fonzie who'd been a regular for over two decades. As soon as I got in the water, we had an immediate connection. I smiled at him, and he smiled back. Actually, dolphins are always smiling; it's how their mouth is shaped. But I took it as a smile intended for me anyway.

The entire time I was snorkeling with Fonzie, he never strayed more than a foot away. He would bump me gently to steer me in a certain direction but would not break eye contact. It seemed as if he was communicating with me.

At the end of what seemed to be only fifteen to twenty minutes, I was told my session was over. I said to the lady in charge that I'd only been in the water for about fifteen minutes. She smiled, then told me I'd been in with him for over an hour, exceeding the forty-five-minute session I'd paid for.

How could this be? Something had happened during this contact, but I wasn't quite sure what it was. Yet.

While driving back home from the Keys, I saw a large sign that read, *New Age Books*. On impulse, I pulled over and bought several books on a variety of topics, including dolphins. For the next couple of months, I found myself steadily ingesting this information. In my research, I learned the experience I'd had with Fonzie was not isolated. It was common among people who swam with dolphins. Many, including me, appear to have a spiritual connection that lingers far beyond the experience itself. I've always believed humans have a profound relationship with the animal kingdom, whether it be with our pets or natural wildlife. To me, the connection is undeniable.

Once my girlfriend and I got settled in after the hurricane and the miraculous encounter with the dolphins, it was time to get back to work to complete my solo album, *Network 23*. First on the agenda was finding a studio. Fortunately, this only took a few days. I found exactly what I needed at New River Studios in downtown Fort Lauderdale, only minutes away from where we lived. This is where I would lay down my guitar solos.

Once this portion of the recording was completed, I had drummer Mike Mangini (as previously mentioned) come in to play on a couple of tracks. While Mike was recording his parts, he mentioned a singer he knew from his hometown of Boston, Scott Gilman. He thought Scott would be a great fit for the project. I got in touch with Scott immediately and had him send me a demo of his vocals. What I heard blew me away! He was not only a great singer, but an exceptional saxophonist as well. Within two days, he was in the studio recording vocal and saxophone parts. He completed writing the lyrics I had started and completed all the vocal and sax parts within the next ten days. Amazing!

Next on the agenda was mixing the album. This process usually takes two days per song. But we ran into a slight obstacle. Guitarist Yngwie Malmsteen (the popular Swedish guitarist) needed the room we were in right away, and he was willing to throw a big chunk of money down to free it up. I knew the owner, Virginia, needed the money, so I agreed to finish the mix as quickly as possible to make the room available.

As it turned out, we had only forty-eight hours. So, the engineer and I spent the next two days straight mixing the album as best we could. In the end, our ears were completely fried. But I was quite impressed with what we'd accomplished in such little time. To my amazement, the mix sounded great.

⚡

With the recording completed, it was time to make copies to shop to different record labels. I hired Marko Babineau, formerly of Geffen Records, to find me a suitable label. He did his best to secure a deal for me, but we kept running into a problem. There was a stigma attached to anyone who'd received recognition as an '80s artist. It was the '90s, and record companies didn't want anything to do with artists of that era, no matter how good their product was. Period.

The record labels wouldn't even listen to my demo. This was not only frustrating for me, but for Marko as well. If it wasn't grunge or a reasonable facsimile, it was off the table. After our relentless dedication and numerous hours of strenuous work, as well as the many obstacles I had to hurdle along the way, I began to realize it was over for this project. All my efforts were for naught.

I was devastated. Not only because of all my hard work resulting in a dead end, but for the money I'd spent. Every penny I had went into this project. Broke with no job prospects or transportation, I was lost in paradise. But the one thing I did have at the end of it all was something I will always treasure: my solo album, *Network 23*. And somehow, that seemed to be enough.

20

Finding My Way Home

Since the cost of completing the album had depleted my savings, I had to find a source of income—and fast! I thought teaching would be the perfect way to remedy this, but after spending a few months desperately searching for students, I finally gave up. Everyone in Florida just wanted to go to the beach, so sitting inside practicing guitar all day was not an option.

I decided to try other avenues to earn a living. First, I tried selling tools over the phone, but after eight hours, I had only sold a screwdriver, and my commission was $1.25. Oh boy, time to celebrate!

While walking home from that promising career opportunity, I spotted one of those blood-drive buses, so I stopped in to donate a couple pints. I earned five dollars in five minutes—four times what I'd made selling stupid tools over the phone for eight hours. I walked to the store and bought a pack of cigarettes and a couple cans of cat food. The cat food was very tasty, and my cat really enjoyed the cigarettes.

My next stab at success came with another telemarketing opportunity. This time, it was selling condoms over the phone to gas stations. Yes, this really happened. The items I was hired to sell were jars of condoms wrapped in gold foil and stamped on both sides to make them look like coins.

They assigned me to the regions of Georgia and Alabama. I had a gut feeling this wasn't going to go well. Sure enough, these greasy gas station rednecks didn't have a clue about what I was trying to sell. They thought I was trying to sell them a condo! They had no idea what a condom was.

Finally, out of frustration, I yelled at one prospective hillbilly client, "It's a fucking rubber, you stupid fucking idiot!"

I was immediately reprimanded and relieved of my rubber-dealing duties.

Since things weren't going very well financially, I sold some of my guitars and amps, as well as most of my recording equipment and collected enough money to drive back to my hometown of Seattle. I hated the thought of leaving Florida, but there was no way to make a living for me there, and there were ample opportunities awaiting in Seattle. This was also the time my girlfriend and I decided to go our separate ways. Such is life.

I rented a moving truck and left for the Pacific Northwest in mid-January of 1997. It was a balmy eighty-two degrees in Fort Lauderdale, and I was well aware this wouldn't be the case where I was headed. The only route feasible for the trek at that time of year was to drive west on Interstate 10 from Florida to California, and then head north on Interstate 5 to Seattle. That way, I could avoid the snow in the upper Midwest and crossing over the Rocky Mountains in mid-winter. This is never a good idea.

With some of the money I'd made from selling my equipment, I purchased a 1984 Renault for $500 so I would have something to drive once I reached Seattle. It turned out to be a major piece of shit. The steering wheel had a lot of play, so you could easily drift into other lanes or off the road if you weren't paying close attention. And when I pushed in on the clutch, the brake would follow, as both were mounted to the same bracket. To the people behind me, it must have looked as if

I was driving while spankin' drunk. But, of course, that wasn't the case. The thing just had a mind of its own.

The French should stick to wine and cheese, as cars are definitely not their forte.

It took seven days to reach my journey's end. Some nights, I drove straight through into the next day. On others, I slept in the truck, as best I could anyway. My cat hated the drive and was bitching the whole way. For her restroom, I set the litter box on the floor in front of the passenger seat. As a result, I was blessed with a not-so-pleasant aroma that accompanied me throughout the seven-day journey, something I wouldn't recommend for the easy queasy.

Once I reached Seattle, I pulled the truck and car trailer in front of my dad's house, where I'd previously arranged to stay for a few days until I found an apartment. When my dad saw me, he bust out laughing. I was disheveled, disoriented, and delirious as I stood in his front yard holding my smelly cat. I grabbed my suitcase and found my way to the guest bedroom, where I slept for the next twelve hours straight, along with my odorous cat with an attitude problem.

I hadn't seen my dad since I stayed with him when filming my instructional video in 1987, ten years earlier, so we had a lot of catching up to do. But first, I wanted to visit my mom and my youngest sister, Sheila, who had Down syndrome. Sheila was hilariously funny. Despite her condition, she was exceptionally sharp-witted and would keep us in hysterics whenever we got together.

After visiting my mom and sister, I returned to my dad's house and found my younger brother Johnny there as well. The boys were back in town! Time to party! We drank, barbequed, reminisced, told stories, and laughed for the next two days. It was the most fun I'd had in a long time. My dad and brother having a similar sense of humor to my own made things very comfortable. It was as if we were long lost friends having a reunion. Communicating with my dad as an adult was quite different compared to the way it was when I was younger. It didn't seem like we were just father and son, we were friends as well. That was a uniquely satisfying place to be. I felt I'd returned home.

In addition to reconnecting with family, I also got reacquainted with some friends from the late '60s and '70s, most being the last people I saw before making my move to Hollywood in 1978. Seeing them again became a marathon of reminiscence, like a high school reunion, except without the high school. As you may recall, I dropped out of the eighth grade, so I skipped the high school part.

❧

Again, another change was on the horizon. I thought it might be time to return to teaching. I really enjoyed sharing my knowledge of music and my unorthodox approach to guitar. The feeling I got watching my younger students become ecstatic when they played their first song was priceless. And seeing my older students become elated when I taught them my two-handed tapping technique was equally satisfying.

I began searching for a place to teach, and within a few days I found a gig at a music store/school in an area called Federal Way, just south of Seattle. Within a month, I had forty students! A bit of an improvement from the three I had in Florida. Just a few months after that, I'd acquired a total of seventy students. I now had enough money to upgrade from that shitty little Renault to something a little nicer. Something that wasn't a death trap. I sold the Renault to a couple of thuggish nineteen-year-old punks for $200. I just wanted to get rid of it, and probably would've paid them to take it.

About two weeks later, there was a thunderous pounding on my door followed by the words: "POLICE! OPEN UP!"

I thought, *WTF?* I opened the door to face several officers in SWAT gear. They burst in, threw me to the floor, and handcuffed me. Damn, what did I do before I left Seattle in 1978?

Turns out the guys I sold that shitty little Renault to had never transferred the title, so it was still registered in my name—and they had just gone on a robbery/shooting spree in Portland, Oregon. While the police were questioning me, they received a call informing them the real suspects had just been apprehended outside of Portland.

What a way to get woken up in the morning!

As the SWAT team was leaving, I requested a defibrillator and a change of underwear. I received a little chuckle for that.

While living in the Pacific Northwest, I really enjoyed the drives I would take down the Oregon coast to Northern California. The Oregon coastline is pristine, with sand dunes and huge rocks that protrude from the shoreline like massive haystacks. (One of them was actually named "Haystack Rock.") The entire coastline is sparsely populated, so you can really appreciate the quiet solitude it has to offer.

While continuing my drive south from Oregon, I entered the redwoods of Northern California. Here, you enter the Land of the Giants, the mighty Sequoia trees. These gentle giants are quite the sight to behold. Some are so enormous in stature that you can drive a car through their base. The eldest date back as far as 1200 BC and have survived numerous forest fires throughout the centuries. Whenever I ventured into this enchanted wonderland, I always took time to park my car, lie on the ground, look upward, and marvel at their magnificence, sometimes for hours at a time.

On one such trip, I cut through the redwoods and headed inland to Mt. Shasta, where I'd made plans to meet my friend Mark and his girlfriend, Thea. After they arrived and checked into the hotel, we drove up to the highest elevation on the mountain accessible by car, which is 9,000 feet. From that vantage point, we could see the multiple colors of the Milky Way. It was as if we could literally reach out and touch the stars. I was awestruck. Or should I say "starstruck?"

Around 11:30 p.m., we found a picnic table where we sat and

sipped some of Mark's homemade wine. From my side of the table, I had a perfect view of the ominous mountain in front of me, as they sat opposite me with their backs toward the mountain.

At the stroke of midnight, a brilliant white flash lit up the entire mountain.

Mark and Thea saw the reflection on my face and quickly looked behind, but the instantaneous flash was gone. They asked what had happened, so I described what I saw. We looked down the mountain toward the road to see if the flash could've been caused by car headlights, but there was no car in sight.

We heard people from other campsites talking about what they'd just witnessed too, and everyone seemed confused about what it was.

Around ten minutes later, another bright flash lit things up. This time it had a blueish hue, and this time, Mark and Thea saw it too. Everyone was now out of their campsites talking about it, not knowing what to make of this mysterious phenomenon.

A few moments later, I looked up at the side of the mountain and saw two lights zig-zagging their way down toward us. It turned out to be a camper carrying a flashlight with another light attached to his helmet.

I asked what he had seen and what he thought may have caused it.

He was visibly shaken. "I've been camping at the same site for the past twelve years, and I've never seen anything like it," he said, throwing his camping gear into the back of his SUV. He hopped into the SUV and tore out of there, spewing gravel in his wake.

A few minutes later, there was another bright flash. This time, it had a pinkish hue. That was followed by a yellow flash and a green flash, all in ten-minute intervals.

People began packing up their tents and heading back down the mountain. The three of us soon followed.

↯

The next morning, as we had breakfast at the Black Bear Diner in the town of Mount Shasta, the whole place was abuzz about the light show.

It was on the front page of all newspapers as far south as Sacramento and broadcast on the morning TV news.

We told some of the locals we were on the mountain when it all happened, and they pelted us with questions: "How bright was it up close? Did you see a UFO? Where did the lights come from?" and on and on. We weren't quite sure how to respond because we didn't know any more than they did. After breakfast, Mark, Thea, and I parted ways. They headed back north toward Seattle, and I headed south toward Sacramento.

For the next several weeks, this extraordinary event occupied my thoughts. What was it that we saw? What caused it?

To this day, no one has proposed a reasonable explanation. The event became known as the Shasta Lights Incident. I felt fortunate to have been there that night to witness the bizarre occurrence. Experiencing strange events and otherworldly phenomena has become the norm for me, and I welcome it with an open mind.

✦

While I was hiking at Discovery Park near Seattle, another strange incident happened, but of a slightly different nature. As I approached the end of the three-and-a-half-hour hike, I noticed clothes strewn alongside the trail. First, a pair of sneakers. Then socks, a shirt, a pair of pants, followed by a bra and panties. I feared a female hiker may have run into some sort of trouble.

A few seconds later, I heard a woman screaming from up the trail, so I took off running in that direction.

What I saw next was the last thing I expected. Two large male cops were holding a woman face down in the grass next to the parking lot. She was completely naked and covered in tattoos.

"Hail, Satan. I am your princess; I am your goddess. Take me!" she screamed repeatedly, all the while struggling fiercely to escape from the cop's unrelenting grasp.

They were having great difficulty restraining her, as she was obviously tweaked on some highly potent hallucinogenic.

I walked up to the officers and informed them her clothes were back on the trail.

As soon as I spoke, she looked up at me with solid black dilated pupils. "Satan, I am your princess," she blurted. "Take me!"

"I'm not Satan," I replied casually. "I'm his nephew, Steve."

At this, she became rather docile and began to grin.

The cops looked at me, stunned.

"What the fuck? How did you do that?" asked one of them.

"It was the only thing I could think of saying," I replied.

"Well, it sure as hell worked!" the other officer said.

The girl was handcuffed, blanketed, and, while still grinning joyfully, was escorted to the police cruiser.

Nephew Steve saved the day!

21

Time for School . . .
and Hot for Teacher

In 2006, the owners of the store where I was teaching informed me that instrument sales were down so low they'd decided to close their doors the following week. I thought, *Oh no, I have seventy students with nowhere to move them. And what about the other teachers, what are they going to do?* This was the time to act, and it became another turning point in the consistently changing adventure I called my life.

Without hesitation, I began looking for a building I could turn into a music school. Within a couple of days, I found the perfect place located only a mile from the store. I quickly signed a lease and had property management section the area into separate rooms. I drew out the floor plan and informed them the rooms had to be soundproofed, that each door to the teaching rooms had to have windows for transparency, the air conditioning ducts had to be rerouted, and at least two electrical outlets had to be installed in each room along with fluorescent lighting. Then I had an alarm installed and bought insurance for the building as well as accident insurance for the students and teachers.

The next step was to furnish the place, so I went shopping at several office outlets and found all the chairs, desks, and tables needed. I also found an art store where I purchased large posters of popular jazz, rock, pop, blues, and classical icons and had them framed. When the interior construction was completed, I moved in the furniture, pictures, and a few plants to give the place a homey atmosphere. I had the name "Federal Way School of Music" painted on the front door and placed an A-board sign advertising the school that I placed out by the street. The last step was to move the pianos, drums, music stands, amplifiers, and teachers' personal effects to their perspective rooms.

And voilà! It was done.

During the last week of teaching at the store, I had the teachers hand out maps with the address of the new school to the students and parents so they could seamlessly continue lessons the following week.

There you have it. I was told the store was closing on a Friday and ten days later had a new school open. Not one of the teachers or students missed a lesson. When all was said and done, I stood out front and thought, *I now own a music school. How cool is that?* And I put it all together while I was still teaching. No wonder I felt like crap. But I also felt very proud. The school would become my main source of income for the next several years and for many of the other teachers as well.

A week after opening the school, my townhouse burned down. Dammit! It all started on August 6, 2006, at 3:00 a.m. I was recording new music in my home studio when a massive explosion shook the building. I ran downstairs with my cat and dashed outside to see what caused it. A large hole had been blown through the wall. An entire side of the building was engulfed in flames—where my adjoining neighbor lived with his wife and kids. I could hear the kids screaming, so I ran over to make sure they all made it out safely. Thankfully, not one of them was injured.

I called 911, but I found there was a problem. The local fire department had already been dispatched to a car fire on the freeway, and the secondary department didn't have our neighborhood on their GPS. I kept hearing the sirens get closer, fade away, get closer, and fade away again. I was confused. The flames were shooting thirty feet above the building with pillars of smoke billowing out. How could they miss that?

About twenty minutes later the firetrucks finally arrived. By this time, my roof was ablaze, and part of it had already collapsed. I didn't understand why the firemen just stood there, having a conversation about what to do. I was dumbfounded. I couldn't believe how nonchalant they were. It was as if they were thinking, *hmmm, that's a nice fire. Where're the marshmallows?*

I ran up to them and yelled, "Look, here's the fire hydrant, you hook up the hose to this, and spray water on the fire. Understand?"

"Anyone still inside?" one of the firemen asked.

"Everyone made it out, including my cat," I replied.

"Is there anything of value inside?" he asked.

"Yes. There are thirty-six guitars and my recording equipment up there." I pointed to the area of my studio which luckily hadn't collapsed yet.

He immediately ran upstairs with another fireman. They grabbed my recording equipment and as many guitars as possible, piled it all into my car and SUV, and then pulled the vehicles out of the garage and parked them down the street.

At that point, I no longer saw them as idiots. They were heroes!

❧

The firemen knew as well as I did what had caused the explosion and subsequent fire. The propane tank attached to my neighbor Cedric's barbecue. When I questioned him about it, he told me he'd been out by the barbecue smoking a cigarette and confessed he threw the lit cigarette by the propane tank where it caught fire due to a leak in the tank. He said he didn't know what to do. So, being drunk on his ass, he ran back inside, hoping it would just go out. *Propane fires don't just go out because you want them to, it doesn't work that way dumbass,* I thought.

So there I was, watching my place burn to the ground while my drunken neighbor ran around, pointing at it and laughing as if he'd created something to be proud of.

Then he walked up to me. "Steve, looks like it's time for a barbecue."

If looks could kill, Cedric would have instantaneously found himself lying in a six-foot hole pushing up daisies with a host of maggots navigating his carcass.

At that moment, the news team from NBC showed up.

Oh boy, more fun! As I stood there, barefoot in my sweatpants and T-shirt, the news reporter began asking questions. I wasn't particularly in the mood for them, especially after the little interlude with Cedric.

After a few questions, she paused and looked at me curiously. "Hey, aren't you the guitar player from Autograph?"

"Yes," I replied and forced a smile.

She then went on to say how much she loved our music and that she used to sing in a high school band that covered our song "Turn Up the Radio."

I was delighted . . . NOT! It was very sweet, but it wasn't the right time to be chatting about her high school escapades. When I saw the news footage the next day, I could see in my facial expression how perplexed I was that we were having this conversation while my home was in flames, crashing to the ground behind me. I mean, really?

The Red Cross showed up shortly thereafter and gave me directions to the hotel where I would stay temporarily. They also handed me a few hundred dollars to hold me over, which is par for the course in these situations. When I arrived at the hotel, the sun was already up. All I wanted to do was go to my room, crawl in bed, and pass out knowing I had to teach in a few hours.

But life wasn't going to be so easy.

As soon as I got to my door, I heard a familiar voice. It was Cedric. I couldn't believe they booked him at the same hotel—in the room next to mine!

When Cedric saw me, he yelled, "Hey Steve, you got any beer? Let's party!"

I envisioned my hands gripping his neck and squeezing with all my might. At that very moment I thought, *I wonder if this is what hell is like?*

22

Lost and Abroad

During the time I taught at my school, I found myself longing to travel again. This time would be much different because I wouldn't be touring with the band or teaching clinics. I'd be sightseeing.

My first excursion took me back to the Netherlands on a non-stop nine-hour flight from Seattle to Amsterdam. The flight path took me over the North Pole where the vast frozen tundra was quite the spectacle.

When I arrived in Amsterdam, they stamped my passport, and I proceeded to baggage claim. After picking up my luggage, I walked out and caught a taxi. But something wasn't quite right. I didn't go through the customary security after I picked up my luggage. I asked the taxi driver why this was.

"What are you going to smuggle into Amsterdam?" he responded in a heavy Flemish accent. "Everything is legal here. When you leave is when you should be concerned."

Made total sense to me.

I stayed at the Bilderberg, a hotel near downtown and close to the Van Gogh and Rijksmuseum. The Bilderberg is famous—or infamous—for hosting the first annual private conference for what became known as the Bilderberg Group, established in 1954. This clandestine group has members from around the globe including political leaders, corporate CEOs, academics, military industrialists, bankers, stock market personnel, and government officials, just to name a few. Critics believe its primary agenda is to control and manipulate Western capitalism and the global marketplace.[6] The hotel where I stayed was not the original where that first meeting took place, but I figured if I stayed at an affiliate, I'd be able to find out more about the original and its historical ties to this highly secretive group, which, as it turned out, was exactly what happened. The staff had most of the answers to my many questions.

＊

What I found interesting in Holland, was that bicycles are the most common way of commuting. They have the right-of-way over cars, buses, and pedestrians. In fact, in many areas, they have their own lane situated between the car and pedestrian lanes with their own traffic lights, which is a symbol of a little bicycle that lights up red or green.

After renting a bike one day, I stopped at one of their famous coffee shops, which was "not" just a coffee shop. Oh, no no no. It was much, much more. Upon entering, they handed me a menu and sat me at a table. At first, I didn't recognize anything on the menu, but after a moment, I realized the items listed were the names for an assortment of marijuana and hashish strains: Purple Haze, White Widow, Super Polm, Skunk, Hashmir . . . there were dozens! I chose the Super Polm. *What the hell, when in Amsterdam, do as those damn Amsterdamers*, I thought. I know I said I'd quit alcohol and drugs back in 1986. But here in 2008, I didn't mind indulging myself in a little alcohol and fugowee. For those of you who don't know what fugowee is, it's my favorite nickname for marijuana. After you smoke or ingest a little, you say: "Where the fugowee?"

6   Joe Sommerlad, "What is the Bilderberg Group and are its members really plotting the New World Order?" Independent, May 28, 2019, https://www.independent.co.uk/news/world/europe/bilderberg-group-conspiracy-theories-secret-societies-new-world-order-alex-jones-a8377171.html.

By the time I left this delightful establishment, I forgot where I parked my bike. I was in no condition to ride anyway and probably would have been hit by a tram or ridden into a canal. So, I walked over to the Hard Rock Cafe and had myself a pint of Heineken, which I thought appropriate, being that it's made in Holland. By the time I finished my beer, I didn't even care where my bike was.

A canal tour was located next to the Hard Rock, and I thought it might be fun. (To be fair, anything was fun in my condition.) Once I sat on the boat, I asked the Japanese man sitting across from me if he'd take my picture, which he happily agreed to do. To return the favor, I took his picture as well. To which he bowed and said, "Hai!" which I undoubtedly was. How did he know?

When I finally got back to my bike, I felt I was straight enough to ride—I know, you don't hear that one very often—so, I went cycling toward Vondelpark. That's Amsterdam's version of NYC's Central Park. As soon as I entered the park, the pungent odor of marijuana permeated the air from every direction. Men and women dressed in business suits smoked pot while a variety of instruments played in the background.

And there was something I didn't expect: a couple having sex, right there, out in the open. I later learned that recreational sex had become legal in the park earlier that day, just so long as the participants were at least 500 meters (1,640 feet) away from the children's playground. I can't imagine this happening at a city park in Alabama or Mississippi. The police or local residents would probably stone them to death. I could imagine them saying, "Damn! What da hell ya thank yer doin? This ain't no Gawden a' Eden."

❧

I really enjoyed Amsterdam's museums, specifically the Van Gogh Museum and Rijksmuseum, which are positioned right next to one another. I'd seen some of Van Gogh's work previously at an exhibit at the Seattle Art Museum (SAM), but it was nothing like what I saw at the actual Van Gogh Museum. It was mesmerizing to see this master's best just a breath away.

Afterward, I walked over to the Rijksmuseum, which houses the works of one of my favorite painters, Rembrandt. I was awestruck observing these masterpieces for the first time close up. Being able to recognize the brushstrokes, the intricate detail, the colors, the shadowing, and the artistic brilliance in his work had a profound effect on me. There's something that strikes your inner core when you witness such magnificent beauty captured by the hand of a true master. It's like a glimpse into the mind and heart of an artistic genius. It changes you in a way you can only feel, not express.

Leaving the Rijksmuseum, I found myself pedaling toward the red-light district. That's right, I was on my way to view an entirely different art form: women in lingerie. As I wandered about sightseeing, I thought it would be cool to get some pictures to share with my friends of the women dancing behind glass while trying to lure prospective customers into their lair. But, as soon as I took out my camera, a man rushed up and yanked it out of my hands.

"What's the problem?" I asked.

"It's strictly forbidden to take pictures of the models," he replied, pointing to the posted signs saying exactly that. "Anyone caught taking a picture will have their camera taken away and it will most likely be disposed of in the canal."

"Why is this so strictly enforced?" I asked.

He told me that many of these women had professional careers as doctors, business owners, lawyers, CEOs, and so on. They fly in from other less fortunate countries to make extra money for a few days. Many of them earn more in the few days they work in Amsterdam than they make in a month at their real profession in their homeland. And circulating pictures of them dancing half naked in a window could compromise or possibly ruin their careers if they were exposed, so to speak.

*

Riding my bike back to the hotel, I noticed something that looked completely out of place. A centuries-old church with a red door sat smack-dab in the middle of the red-light district. And yes, it was still in service.

I thought, *Now I've seen it all—legal drugs, coffee houses that rolled joints for you, sex in the park, women in lingerie dancing in windows, canals filled with bicycles from drunkards, and a church in the middle of a red-light district.*

There's nothing not to love about Amsterdam.

*

The next day, I checked out of the hotel and boarded a train to attend the Pink Pop Festival in southern Holland near the Belgian border. Several bands were playing the event, with Metallica as the headliner. Earlier, when I'd tried to book a hotel for the event, there was nothing available. Fortunately, I found a castle not far from the festival grounds that had one vacant room left. Yes, you read that right. A castle.

As the taxi from the train station pulled up to my new temporary residence, my jaw dropped. This castle was complete with a moat, drawbridge, garden terrace, and circular towers with spires mounted atop. And the room I reserved had a view of it all. The suite was especially large, with a king bed made for a king, wood-beamed ceilings, and the original antique floors and furniture to keep its authenticity.

The following day, I had lunch on the terrace and caught a taxi to the festival. While there, I stood in the crowd and listened to a few bands before people started to recognize me from Autograph. I don't usually mind this, but, in this instance, it was a bit overwhelming. People attempted to communicate with me in a variety of languages, and some were even getting aggressive, demanding guitar picks or some kind of memento.

Luckily, a lady I'd worked with while doing clinics in Holland several years prior recognized me and escorted me away from the mob. I sat with her at a small makeshift café on the outskirts of the crowd and bought her a glass of wine to thank her for coming to the rescue. Shortly thereafter, it began to rain, so I decided to head back to the hotel. I kindly thanked my savior again for helping me out and bid her farewell.

Returning to the hotel turned out to be a daunting endeavor, as many other festival goers were also trying to leave because of the unexpected weather change. Taxis became extinct within minutes. After waiting for about an hour for another taxi to arrive, I decided to walk to the nearest town to find one that could take me back to my hotel. This didn't work very well, especially since no one spoke English in this remote part of Holland. Asking them to call a taxi was about as fruitless as asking a dog for directions to the zoo.

So, there I was again, a stranger in a strange land, soaking wet, shivering, lost, unable to speak the language, buzzed on wine, and hungry. Just another typical day in my life.

Eventually, a taxi drove by, and I flagged him down. Since he didn't understand English well, I showed him a book of matches with the name of the hotel on it.

"Ah, yes," he said.

Ten minutes later, I was at home in my castle. Upon arrival, I went straight to my room to dry off and change. I then went downstairs to the dungeon, where the bar was (appropriately) located, but it was closed to the public for a private party celebrating an employee's retirement. The man of honor saw me at the entrance, and we recognized each other. He had been my waiter at lunch that day.

When he saw I was being turned away, he addressed the doorman. "No, no, no. This is my friend, Steve from America, and I want him to join us."

I felt honored when he took me in and introduced me to his wife, kids, parents, co-workers, and friends. We ate, drank, and laughed for the remainder of the evening, with me not understanding what they were saying most of the time. But I've found that when you're smiling and laughing, there are no language barriers.

When I caught the train back to Amsterdam the next day and flew back home, I was grinning all the way. That is, until I arrived at the airport in Seattle. The taxi driver who initially picked me up was right: you don't have to worry about customs when arriving in Amsterdam; it's when you leave is when you should be concerned.

Sure enough, as I was going through customs in Seattle, they took one glance at me and, being the long-haired musician-type traveling alone and arriving from the drug mecca of Europe, they instructed me to follow the blue line. That meant I was going to be searched. Big time. Now, I'm not going into detail about what happened in that little interrogation room they escorted me to, but when they finished, I felt violated.

Afterward, I asked if they wanted to share a cigarette, to which they unsuccessfully tried to contain their laughter.

✦

My next adventure brought me to Cancun, Mexico. For many years, I longed to visit the Mayan ruins of Chichen Itza and Tulum. When I got to the hotel, I was pleased to see that my room had a stunning view of the Gulf of Mexico. I took it all in for a while. Then I toured the town and soaked up some sun on the beach with a few cocktails. That was the life!

After a few days of relaxation, I decided it was time to visit those Mayan ruins of Chichen Itza. The charter bus from Cancun to the ruins was a beautifully scenic three-hour drive. As soon as we arrived, the tour guide warned that the bus would be departing at precisely 5:00 p.m. so we better not split from the group. Being the rebel I am, I promptly split from the group once the tour began and went on my own picture-taking expedition.

The tour guide saw me as I was leaving. "Remember," he shouted, " we leave at 5:00 p.m. sharp, señor, whether you're on the bus or not. And the next bus back to Cancun isn't until 1:00 p.m. tomorrow."

I assured him I would be back in time, which, of course, I wasn't.

As I traipsed around this magnificent wonderland, gazing in awe at the pyramids, the observatory, and several other fascinating structures, I noticed more ruins beyond the fenced tourist area. And so, being a dumbass, I ignored the warning signs and ventured into the jungle by myself, snapping pictures of whatever piqued my curiosity along the way. I didn't realize these ruins covered an enormous amount of real estate, making it very easy to lose your way, or get eaten by something.

After a couple of hours spent roaming aimlessly, I stopped to look around. I had no idea where I was, but I did know one thing for certain: I was lost . . . in the jungle . . . in the middle of the Yucatan Peninsula . . . and the bus was leaving in a half hour.

"Shit!" I started running back the way I thought I'd come, but ended up going in the wrong direction, which I later found out was away from the bus's location.

Luckily, I found a hotel, in the middle of nowhere. I ran inside. "Where are the tour buses parked? I have only five minutes to make it back."

The person behind the front desk just looked at me and shook his head. "It will take you at least an hour to walk back to the site, and we don't have a shuttle to take you there."

He told me the only other option was to run back through the jungle the way I'd come, which would take about twenty-five minutes. But that came with the risk of getting lost again. I opted for that approach anyway and ran through the jungle as fast as I could.

Amazingly, I found the parking lot to find only one bus left. As I got closer, I could read the destination sign in front: *Cancun*. Yes! It was my bus!

As soon as I approached, the tour guide stepped off the bus. "We've been waiting for twenty minutes and were just about to leave."

I apologized and graciously thanked him for waiting, explaining that I'd gotten lost. Once I entered the bus, I apologized to everyone else for being late. A few sneers and disgruntled remarks floated toward me, but they were in Spanish and German, so I didn't understand them anyway.

I casually walked back to my seat, smiling as though they were complimenting me. And when I sat down, I got a big surprise. They all applauded. They weren't mad. They were happy I'd made it back safely, as was I.

❧

The next day, I set off on yet another adventure, this time to the Mayan ruins of Tulum. This time, I was NOT going to stray from the tourist area. I'd already learned my lesson the hard way. The ruins of Tulum were some of the most picturesque scenes I'd ever laid eyes upon. They sat atop a cliff above the white sands and turquoise waters of the Caribbean. The glistening white structures of the ruins were surrounded by palm trees, lush greenery, and sun-bleached sand trails that stretched out in every direction. That site had been beautifully preserved over millennia, marred only by the impact of natural elements over time.

While strolling around, taking in the sites and snapping pictures, I ran into a familiar looking elderly couple. I recognized them from the bus that had taken us to Chichen Itza the day before.

"Don't get lost," they said.

We simultaneously broke out laughing at that, and I assured them that was *not* on my agenda.

They were the sweetest people imaginable, and we found ourselves engaged in a very enjoyable conversation straight away. They were from Idaho. I informed them that I, too, hailed from the Pacific Northwest. We sat and ate our lunches together under the shade of palm trees, chatting away, sharing wine, and admiring the breathtaking views around us. It was another reminder that it's not only the incredible things you witness in your travels that make it so special, but the people you meet along the way.

❧

As I left the Tulum site, I noticed a huge iguana. It noticed me too—and not in a friendly way. For no apparent reason, this alligator-sized lizard ran straight at me. I didn't know if he wanted to eat me or fuck me, but I assure you, I ran as fast as I could. All my fellow tourists pointed and laughed at this fiasco. The creature chased me all the way to the charter bus and didn't stop until I got on. This thing was unrelenting. Why me? What are the odds? There were a lot of other people walking around, why wasn't Godzilla attacking them?

As I looked out the window of the bus, the Jurassic-Park-wannabe just stood there, staring and sticking its tongue out as if mocking me. As I sat there looking back at him, I fantasized about iguana shoes, with matching pants.

23

The Cost of Rica

Initially, I wanted to visit Costa Rica to look for vacation property to purchase. That changed following my first night there. After arriving at the airport in the capital city of San José and passing through customs, I walked out front to hail a taxi. As I waited, I noticed customs agents as well as heavily armed police, drug-sniffing dogs, and military personnel everywhere, as if they were expecting a political coup. Since I'd already done my research regarding the trip, I knew the hotel was only fifteen minutes from the airport. So, when I informed the driver which hotel I was staying at, I didn't expect it to take more than twice that long.

"The hotel is only fifteen minutes from the airport," I finally said. "Why is it taking so long to get there?"

He turned around and gave me an angry look. "We are almost there, señor. Be patient." Then he muttered something in Spanish to himself

It was obvious this *Tico* was taking me for a ride, literally and figuratively.

While peering out the rear passenger window, I saw a hostile-looking character with his shirt off, covered in tattoos, holding a machete across his shoulders. As we passed by, he glared at me with a demonic look as if I were his next victim.

Boy, I'm sure glad I'm not staying in this crime-infested hellish neigh-borhood, I thought.

Twenty yards farther, we pulled into the hotel.

Damn! This is going to be my hood for the next ten days?

It was shortly after 10:00 p.m. when we arrived, so the kitchen had just closed. I was famished, since I hadn't eaten since the plane departed Seattle twelve hours earlier. After checking into my room, I went down to ask where I could walk to get something to eat. They cautioned me that it was too dangerous to walk around that area at night so called me a taxi. Gee, I wonder why? Could it be because José the machete man was standing just out front, waiting to filet me?

When the taxi arrived, I asked him to take me to the nearest decent restaurant that was open. After driving for twenty minutes, he pulled into a gravel parking lot with a building in the back that was lit up like a micro-casino. It didn't exactly look like your typical family diner. Sure enough, I walked in and, lo and behold, it was a strip club.

As you may have surmised, most strip clubs don't offer the most exquisite dining selection. I wanted sirloin tips and brussels sprouts, not tenderloin tits and bushy sprouts. I was so hungry at this point that I thought, *What the hell. I'll see what they have to eat anyway.*

As soon as I sat down, I ordered a glass of wine and asked for a menu. It was just a half page and, of course, written in Spanish. Within thirty seconds, a stripper sat down next to me and motioned for me to buy her a drink.

"No," I replied, pointing to the menu and my mouth, indicating I just wanted to eat.

At that moment, the bartender walked up and placed a martini in front of her.

"I didn't order that," I said. I immediately asked him for the check and to call me a taxi. The check was forty dollars. I was *not* happy. I didn't even have time to enjoy my wine. I paid the bill after a little bickering and left without tipping.

While I waited outside for the taxi, it began to rain. When I say rain, I mean of the monsoon variety. I waited and waited until I finally realized the bartender hadn't called a taxi. So, I asked the doorman to call me one, but he acted as if he didn't understand what I was talking about. I pulled out a twenty-dollar bill and handed it to him, and from that point on, he miraculously understood English. Imagine that! He called me a cab, and within five minutes, it arrived, and I was outta there.

I finally laid down to get some sleep around 3:00 a.m. Just as I was falling asleep, BAM! BAM! Gunshots. They came from a Caribbean bar across the street from the hotel. From what I was told, the local Ticos don't like the Caribbean Costa Ricans, so they're always at war with one another.

As I peered out my window, I spotted the victim lying on his back with blood running from his lifeless body down the street and into a storm drain.

How barbaric, I thought. *No one seems to even care.*

When the police and ambulance showed up about fifteen minutes later, they acted as if it was no big deal. While the paramedics nonchalantly checked the body, the police just stood around chatting with the patrons from the bar, drinking beer and smoking cigarettes.

Wow. I hope I don't get shot in this place.

Well, to be honest, I hope I don't get shot *anywhere!*

❧

First thing the next morning, I called the realtor with whom I was scheduled to view some properties and canceled our appointment. I'd seen enough. There was no way I was going to purchase anything in this place. After that first night, I decided to just be a tourist and enjoy the sights.

Most American, Canadian, and European tourists don't realize that when you book a vacation through a travel agency, you get picked up from the airport in an air-conditioned charter bus and brought to an American-owned resort, so you're not actually seeing the reality of the country you're visiting. But when you venture out by yourself—which I usually do—you'll realize it can be quite different from what you'd envisioned. This is something you will *not* find in any fancy travel brochure.

↯

I decided my next outing should be with a tour group. It started out with a charter bus picking me and a few others up from the hotel. We were headed to Mount Arenal, an active volcano three hours northwest of San José, where our hotel was located. The drive there was breathtaking. Costa Rica certainly does not lack in its natural beauty.

Upon arriving at the resort, which was located at the base of the volcano, I could see Arenal smoldering in the background from a recent eruption. It felt as though I'd entered into a pre-historic era. I wouldn't have been the least bit surprised if a gigantic Tyrannosaurus Rex suddenly appeared and came running at me. In fact, I would have considered it an appropriate sequel to being chased by that giant lizard in Mexico.

For the next two days, I became lost in the magnificence of this jungle paradise and took full advantage of all the perks the luxurious resort offered. The food, people, hospitality, environment, and amenities made this part of my trip exceptional. I didn't want to leave. But this part of my adventure had come to an end, and it was time for the next.

When I returned to the hotel, I decided to rent a car and drive to the Pacific coast on the west side of Costa Rica. The concierge at the front desk had a recommendation for me. His cousin owned a car rental business located close to the hotel and was happy to give me a discount.

Now, for those of you who aren't privy to such an experience, everyone says they have a cousin or uncle who will gladly "cut you a deal" in Costa Rica. But that's not the case. The concierge's "cousin" came to the hotel and picked me up an hour later. He brought me to his rental lot and chose the car for me; I had no say. He told me the price for the old beaten-up silver Nissan Sentra was seventy-five dollars a day, which I thought was outrageous. When I checked with Alamo, their cost was twenty-eight dollars a day for a new car, including full-coverage insurance.

When I mentioned this to the concierge's cousin, he said there were no cars available because of some holiday. (I later found out there was no such holiday.) Go figure. At that point, I wasn't going to squabble. I just wanted to get something to drive and be on my way.

While he was getting the paperwork together, he informed me the insurance was not included—surprise, surprise—and that, if the car were stolen, the insurance I purchased from him would not cover it. In addition to that, the car had no hubcaps (which I made sure he was aware of), and there was only a half tank of gas (which I also pointed out), as well as a dent in the passenger side door. Yup, I had a real winner.

He then gave me a special lock, one which is quite common there. It connects from the steering wheel to the five-speed gear shift. (They didn't have any automatics available—again, I wasn't surprised).

"You must use the lock, even if you just stop to use a restroom," he said. "And keep driving if you get a flat tire. If you don't, the locals will rob you blind, take the car, and leave you on the side of the road with nothing."

The best thing to do in case of a flat tire, apparently, was to keep driving on the flat until I reached a gas station and wait till morning to buy a new one. The car didn't come with a spare in the trunk; it was already on the car.

He pulled out a map and started circling landmarks for directions.

"Why can't I just follow the signs?" I asked.

"There aren't any. People steal them to patch holes in their roofs."

My confidence in this endeavor had now shrunk to nil. But I decided since I was this far in, why not finish? What did I have to lose, right?

I was amazed that I was able to navigate all the way to the Pacific in that little piece of shit deathtrap with the makeshift map of circled landmarks. I guess my spirit guides were with me that day. As I continued driving down the coastline, I found a beautiful, American-owned resort right on the water and checked in straight away. I had a delicious seafood dinner and ordered a bottle of wine to take to the beach that evening. As I sat on the beach drinking my wine, I gazed up at the constellations and listened to the sound of the waves gently lapping the shore. *Ahhh,* I was in paradise and, surprisingly, still alive.

The next morning, I arose early to continue my voyage south toward Manuel Antonio National Park. I asked the concierge at the front desk if he could recommend any zip-line adventures in the direction I was headed. As one might expect, his "cousin" owned one right down the road and would gladly give me a discount.

There I go again.

Now, if you're unfamiliar with zip-lining, it involves a network of cables connected to trees that start from a high elevation and relay down to the bottom. To use the zipline, you connect a clasp to the cable while you're strapped into a harness, then slide from tree to tree down a mountain, using a thick leather glove on the cable as your brake. If you don't brake in time, you smash into the next tree—which I quickly discovered. If you brake too soon, you will stop between trees and have to pull yourself to the next, risking that someone will come crashing into you from behind—which I also found out) I later learned that locally owned zip-line companies didn't have safety regulations like the American-owned ones. You're pretty much on your own after jumping from that first tree, something I wish I'd known beforehand.

To make things more exciting, it was very windy that day, causing the trees to be tossed wildly about as though I were in the middle of a tropical typhoon. That can make it very difficult when you're on a tiny platform undoing the clasp from one cable and attaching it on the next with no guardrails and a hundred-foot drop.

Oh yeah, my kind of adventure.

NOT!

I became a different kind of tree hugger that day. All the way down the mountain, which took sixteen separate cables, I heard people screaming behind me. They were not having fun. I was the first in the group to reach the bottom, and, thankfully, everyone else eventually made it down safely as well. At the end of the experience, the tour guide asked if anyone would like to do it again. In unison, everyone emphatically replied with a resounding, "NO!"

After that adventure, I got back into my luxurious sedan—with the dented door, no hubcaps, no spare, bald tires, and the fuel gauge next to empty—and continued my journey. Just before I reached the popular surfing town of Jaco, I had to cross a makeshift bridge since the original had been washed away from a flash flood. The local "engineers" had placed two steel beams across the steep ravine to keep the traffic flowing. Each beam was only about two feet wide, so it was only meant for one vehicle to cross at a time.

While I was traversing the bridge, a large truck in front of me stopped halfway across. It didn't look good. As I was peering over the side at the 300-foot drop, the truck began to move, shaking the beams violently and causing the Sentra to bounce uncontrollably.

This is it, I thought. *This little piece of shit car is going to be my coffin at the bottom of this ravine!*

Making it even more fun, it was raining so hard that I couldn't see ten feet in front of me. So, who would notice if a little silver-colored sarcophagus slipped off into the abyss?

Thankfully, a few moments later, the truck made it across, and I made it to the other side too, without incident. Phew! For the second time in a three-hour period, I thought I was going to be trading in my guitar for a harp—or a pitchfork—or whatever.

As I continued driving south, I started to get tired and decided to find a hotel for the night. The rain had finally subsided as I drove into a little coastal town called Quepos, where I found a quaint little hotel just off the main road. The sun was beginning to set, so I thought it would be nice to watch it from the beach. But when I walked across the street to the beach, I found it was completely covered in garbage. There was literally no clean place to stand or sit. Disappointed, I went back to the hotel, had dinner, and went to bed.

After I awoke the next morning, I went in search of a café for breakfast. As I walked down the main street, I couldn't help but notice the heaps of trash piled in vacant lots. The stench was putrid. I passed by a large pile beside the sidewalk and saw a stray dog, so I paused for a moment to see what this poor, mangled thing was eating. Whatever it was, this dog was ferociously devouring it as though its life depended on it, which was most likely the case. I wished I hadn't stopped because, on closer inspection, I saw that the dog was ripping the flesh from another dog's lifeless skull.

Obviously, this ruined my appetite, so breakfast was not an option any longer. As I forced myself not to vomit, I made my way back to the hotel and checked out.

While driving away from Quepos, I thought of the term, "It's a dog-eat-dog world." That saying turned out not to be just a figure of speech, it was reality. And I just witnessed it firsthand.

Manuel Antonio National Park was only fifteen minutes south of Quepos, but completely opposite of where I'd just been. How could such a pristine environment with its lush tropical jungle and white sandy beaches exist next to what felt like a post-apocalyptic war zone? I was perplexed.

Regardless, I chose to get the most out of my day and enjoy everything this picturesque slice of nature had to offer.

As I followed the cliff-side trail overlooking the beach for a few miles into the park a monkey jumped from tree to tree alongside me. We became friends after I left some trail mix for him, which I thought appropriate considering I was on a "trail." (Okay, enough of that.) After a few hours of walking about in this idyllic paradise, I decided it was time to head back to the car. But when I got there, I saw a problem.

Since I'd been gone, the tide had come in. It filled the small bay I'd walked across earlier, and the last boat carrying tourists back to the parking lot had just left.

I'd literally missed the boat.

Oh Boy, I thought. *I get to spend the night on Gilligan's Island with this friggin' monkey that ate all my trail mix and cornbread!*

The little bastard was still in a tree just above my head, squealing for more handouts. (As you may have surmised, the yin and yang in my life are pretty consistent.)

Miraculously, just a few moments later, a park ranger appeared from the trail and saw me standing there with the annoying primate grabbing at my hair from above. He informed me the last boat had left already (which I already knew) and that I couldn't stay in the park. Like I really wanted to?

"You know, there are 120 different species of snakes in Costa Rica," he said, "But only twenty-two are poisonous. Many of the poisonous ones claim this area as their habitat."

Lucky me. I wish they would've told me this earlier, before I went traipsing around through the jungle cluelessly.

After sharing his venomous wisdom, the park ranger radioed the boat to come back and pick me up. They charged twenty dollars for that. I had a sneaky suspicion they were "cousins" as well.

❧

Once I got back to the car, I felt I'd had enough excitement for the day and drove back to San José. When I arrived, it was dark, and I had no idea which exit to take to the hotel. After exiting onto what I thought might be the right one, nothing looked familiar. I asked a taxi driver if he could show me the way to the hotel, but he was busy.

"I'll radio my cousin. He's just a few minutes away."

Oh no, here we go again, more cousins, I thought. Everyone in Costa Rica must be related. It's oddly reminiscent of America's south.

When his supposed cousin arrived, I followed him around for about twenty minutes until he finally pulled into the hotel. I could see the freeway exit from the front of the hotel, so I'd only been a few blocks away. When I informed the driver of this, he started arguing with me in Spanish—conveniently forgetting he spoke English. I threw up my hands and paid him twenty dollars. At this point, I felt I needed to find some cousins of my own here before I went broke.

The next morning, when I returned the rental car, it had a half tank of gas. Just the way it was when I picked it up. Of course, the manager argued with me about it and said he was going to charge me four dollars per gallon to fill the tank.

"There were hubcaps on it when you picked it up," he hollered. "And there was no dent in the door."

By that time, I was angry, which for me takes a lot. "I'm not paying for those ridiculous charges," I said.

He didn't reply. He just printed out the receipt and called a taxi to take me back to the hotel.

When I arrived, I had the concierge at the front desk translate the receipt for me. Sure enough, he charged my card for all the things he wasn't supposed to.

At that point, I was getting used to the way certain things worked here, so I knew what to expect.

⚡

The next day I decided to take a walk into the city center, just ten blocks away. I figured I'd be safe walking in the neighborhood so long as I got back before nightfall, when machete man was on the prowl.

The city center was clean and beautifully ornate. Statues sat everywhere among the old Spanish architecture, making it seem as if they were a natural feature. I spent the day visiting the little shops, had lunch at a quaint sidewalk café, and snapped pictures of this curiously attractive place. The townspeople were gracious and courteous. Some spoke English very well and laughed when I shared my misadventures of the previous days. They told me there were some bad people in the undesirable neighborhoods—same as anywhere. Tourist must be careful of being taken advantage of, especially if they're alone.

Point taken. I'd already experienced it.

After an enjoyable day, I began my walk back to the hotel. Prior to arriving, a big Caribbean Costa Rican grabbed my shirt and pulled me into a narrow alleyway. I struggled until I finally broke free and took off running as fast as possible. I looked back to see he'd pulled out a knife and was rushing toward me. I thought I was a goner! But he stopped short just a block up, turned around, and started running in the opposite direction.

I didn't know why, but I was incredibly relieved. And then I saw a sign a little farther up the street. It said "Policia." I still wonder what would've transpired if that police station hadn't been there.

When I returned to my hotel room, I locked the door and collapsed onto the bed. It was my last day, and I couldn't wait to fly home. But later that night—BAM BAM! I was awoken at 3:00 a.m. by gunshots from the club across the street. Again. That time, I didn't even bother to get up and look out the window. I just turned over and went back to sleep.

❧

The next morning, I took a taxi to the airport and boarded my flight home. While traveling, I thought about all the craziness I experienced during this mission of mayhem. Corrupt taxi drivers, machete man, a strip club "diner," Caribbean street murder, a jalopy rental shyster, navigating by landmarks, death-wish zip-lining, a treacherous bridge crossing, garbage town, dogs eating dogs, a psycho monkey stalker, missing the boat, being mugged by a homeless man, and another murder. I'd seen it all.

I wasn't on vacation; I was making an Indiana Jones movie.

Once I arrived home and walked out the front doors of the Seattle-Tacoma Airport, I literally got down on my knees and kissed the ground. Then I called my cousin to come pick me up.

Just kidding, I don't have a cousin in Seattle. They're all in Costa Rica.

24

Wait; Which One of You is Me?

By 2009, the social media craze was taking over. At the top of the list was Facebook, a place where people could fool anyone by creating fictitious characters. This site, along with other social media sites, can be addicting and cause sleep deprivation, depression, anxiety, cyberbullying, isolation, and infidelity, to name a few.

Personally, I thought it would be a good way to connect with friends and family I'd lost contact with over the years, which it did—and very well, I might add. But after using Facebook for just over a year, I began to feel it was a bit intrusive and decided to shut it down. It just wasn't for me.

I didn't reactivate it until a few years later. It was against my better judgment, but I realized how valuable social media was for marketing and promotion. After a time, I began to really enjoy it. If used properly, I found it had many advantages, like the ability to communicate with people around the world instantaneously. In fact, social media platforms offer the only way do so so other than by phone or email.

Soon after reactivating Facebook, I received an unexpected message from a fan. She informed me of a guy who was claiming to be me in LA. Funny thing is, she believed *he* was the real Steve Lynch and that *I* was the fraud.

What?

His first name was Steve, and he played guitar, so I guess that qualified him to be me. Huh? I asked her to take a close look at the old and new photos of myself I'd posted on my Facebook page to do a comparison. I then requested that she ask him to perform the lead part from "Turn Up the Radio" or my solo "Hammerhead" the next time she saw him.

A week later, she sent another message telling me he couldn't do either. In fact, he got a little pissy when she asked and said he didn't play "Autograph" shit anymore.

Oh my, I wonder why? Could it be because he wasn't capable?

It was identity theft of the musical variety. The weird thing is, this guy was six foot five, and I'm five foot eight. He was creepy looking as well, way creepier than me. She told me he was always seen around the LA hot spots getting drunk on free drinks and picking up women while pretending to be me. He was having drinks bought for him and getting laid by women under my name? How dare he! That's my job, dammit! (Just kidding. Kinda). I guess by intentionally staying out of the limelight and becoming a bit of a recluse, I'd left the door open to impostors.

But it gets even stranger from there. This guy refused to acknowledge he wasn't me. Really? I'd had enough. I decided to contact my long-time friend and attorney, Rob, to track him down and find out who he really was. Which he did.

Rob immediately sent the impostor a letter to cease and desist. But to no avail. Eventually, I took a trip down to LA and made a few appearances at my old haunts to prove my authenticity, which was very weird. Proving I am *me*? As soon as people saw me, they knew who I was. So, it was official: I proved him to be an impostor.

His demented little game skidded to an abrupt halt. From what I understand, he wasn't seen around much after that. And I think the free booze and women were pretty much out of the question as well. Poor guy. I wonder if he moved to Vegas and became an Elvis impersonator.

⚡

A few months after this fiasco, I received another unexpected message on Facebook. This time, it was a girl saying her boyfriend was professing to be me. And again, she thought it was me who was the impostor. I was beginning to doubt if I really was me. And, of course, his name was Steve, and he played guitar. So, I guess it could have been me?

Wait, I think I'm losing it a little. Now *I'm* confused.

This impostor was only five foot two inches. I guess he was the mini-me version. Again, I had to go through the whole charade of asking his girlfriend to check his ID, look at my pictures for comparison, and have him play some of my guitar solos, which, of course, he refused.

So, are there any more of me out there? Please come forward now. I need to keep track of who is me.

Sheesh!

25

Goodbye, Dear Friends

All good things must pass. Sadly, on December 9th, 2008, my good friend and keyboardist of Autograph, Steve Isham, passed away. He'd been fighting cancer for several years, but in the end, had succumbed to it. He was one of the most genuine people I'd ever met, and there was nothing he wouldn't do for anyone. The keyboard parts he came up with and his songwriting style had a unique sound that played a huge part in Autograph's success.

❧

Years later, on April 28th, 2017, my friend and Autograph drummer, Keni Richards, also passed. He met with a tragic and violent end. He was shot twice in the abdomen and bled to death at his home in Palm Desert, California. His friends, as well as the police, believe it was over a drug deal gone bad. Whatever the case may be, Keni did not deserve to go out this way.

In the end, all those who knew Steve Isham thought of him as being funny, friendly, down to earth, compassionate, and determined, as well as an incredibly talented keyboardist, singer, songwriter, and performer. As far as Keni goes, well, Keni was Keni. One of a kind. He was hilariously funny, flamboyant, unpredictable, creative, talented, and crazy as hell! Each of them had individual characteristics that were magnetic to whoever came within their sphere. I miss them, as do their families, friends, and anyone whose lives they touched. I'll see you again one day, my brothers. RIP.

26

Lynch Licks . . . and the Pain

While I was managing my music school, writing music, and traveling about on international escapades, I wrote an online teaching course called Lynch Licks. It took a tremendous amount of work to put this site together. It consisted of filming 100 short videos of me playing various guitar licks along with eighteen guitar solos, explaining each step by step. I had to get everything done over one weekend because the videographer, Ian, and the sound engineer, Chad, had other commitments the following Monday. This not only put stress on me mentally, but it was also murder on my hands. After fourteen hours that Saturday, we finished all 100 licks. I was happy it was completed in one day, but my hands were not.

The next day, I videotaped the eighteen guitar solos. For this, I had to play each solo along with the accompanying music, and then demonstrate each section of the solo while explaining the theory behind it. Each solo took numerous attempts to video and several more takes with the explanations to get it down perfectly. But we got it done. And this time, it took only eleven hours.

By the time I loaded all my guitars into my car, I began to notice how the relentless marathon of guitar butchery over the past two days was affecting me. My finger joints ached, and my hands and forearms were beginning to swell and cramp. When I went back into the studio to say goodbye to Ian and Chad, both said they couldn't believe I just played guitar for twenty-five hours in two days. I was so burned out I could barely respond. I just stood there staring at them blankly with my Gumby-like arms hanging at my sides.

As I drove home, my arms and hands cramped to the point that it became difficult to steer, so I pulled off to the side of the freeway and waited for them to uncramp. By the time I finally reached my house, the pain was so severe I struggled to open the car door. At that moment, I realized I may have caused some serious damage.

As it turned out, I had.

After a night of downing ibuprofen and putting ice packs on my arms, I finally got a few hours of sleep. The first thing I did when I awoke the next morning was call my hand specialist, Dr. Sandboldt. He demanded I come to his office for an emergency evaluation. The news was *not* good, and he was *not* happy. The doctor had operated on my hands previously, so he was well aware of what I'd done to cause these problems again.

❧

My hand issues all started in the summer of 1998. After breaking my right wrist in a fall, I drove to the nearest emergency room where they took X-rays and found I'd broken both wrist bones. The doctor had to reset my hand to my arm and cast it right away, but he warned me the cast alone may not be enough, considering the severity of the break. Apparently, my hand was attached to my arm by tendons only, which meant it may not set properly with just a cast. This didn't sit well with me. And to be quite honest, I was scared. Really scared,

Six weeks later, when the cast was removed, I looked down at my arm in horror. My hand was about a quarter inch below my wrist. The bones hadn't fused correctly, so they were barely connected. The doctor informed me it had to be re-broken and reset using traction to hold it in place while it healed. Hearing this, I almost fainted. He told me it would require a surgeon to correct it. He referred me to Dr. Sandboldt and called him right away to explain the situation. Dr. Sandboldt said I needed to come in ASAP for emergency surgery or I might lose the use of my right hand.

I thought my guitar playing days were over.

The very next day, I lay on an operating table counting backward from ten. But there was a slight problem. The anesthetic didn't knock me out completely, and due to the effect of the anesthetic, I was unable to inform them. What I experienced next was the most excruciating pain I could've ever imagined. I could feel them breaking the wrist bones and drilling holes into my hand and arm bones to insert the metal traction rods. During the procedure, I was in and out of consciousness for about two hours, and believe me, it was *not* fun.

While coming out of the anesthesia, the pain kept getting worse. And no matter how much morphine they administered; it would not subside. It was so severe I was literally passing out, coming back to consciousness, then passing out again. They finally gave me something that completely knocked me out and kept me overnight under observation.

Before I was released the next morning, they gave me explicit instructions to follow for the next eight weeks while my hand was in traction. First, they told me I couldn't use it for anything. Period. I was to tape a plastic bag around my hand and wrist when showering, which is no easy feat to accomplish with one hand. I also had to unwrap the gauze bandage, cleanse the areas where the rods were inserted, and re-bandage it twice a day.

As I repeated this process daily, I noticed my wrist getting smaller and smaller from lack of use. In fact, my whole arm was dwindling to nothing. I knew I faced a long road ahead with rehabilitation. And the worst part was not knowing whether I'd ever play guitar again.

Finally, after eight weeks, Dr. Sandboldt removed the rods. He prescribed physical therapy, which I was to follow for the next six months to stretch the tendons and build the muscles back up.

Lastly, he delivered some grim news. "It's very unlikely you'll be playing guitar again. If you do, your mobility will be restricted, and your playing skills won't be what they once were."

I refused to accept his prognosis. "I'm going to make a full recovery and come back better than ever," I said.

He just shook his head and grinned at the same time, admiring my determination but probably thinking this wasn't plausible.

It took a year from the time I'd broken my wrist to the time I could finally start playing again. I had to relearn how to hold a pick and re-train my right hand to play my two-handed tapping technique. It was like starting over. But after another two years of intense practicing, I was back to where I'd once been. For me, this wasn't good enough. I wanted to be *better* than I was. So, I kept up my practice regimen of four to five hours a day. This turned out to be a big mistake and led to another problem. I developed carpel tunnel in my left hand, which meant I had to revisit Dr. Sandboldt for another operation.

When I went into his office for the evaluation, I could tell he wasn't any happier to see me than I was to see him. He knew I'd done exactly what he told me NOT to do. Fortunately, though, a carpel tunnel operation is a fairly simple procedure. They made an incision in my palm, severed a tendon, and after a few weeks, I was able to start practicing again.

But this time, I decided to play it safe: I cut my practice time down to just two hours a day.

I've always had problems with my hands. I repeatedly had to change my playing technique by holding my pick differently and angling my hands so they wouldn't cramp or hurt when playing. While I was attending the Guitar Institute, I had to change my technique twice in one year because of the pain and cramping. So, it's basically been a career-long ordeal. But I now know when to back off, which brings me back to why Dr. Sandboldt was so upset when I came back several years later for emergency surgery after my marathon weekend of recording the Lynch Licks site. He had warned me many times not to overdo it, and this time, I'd *really* overdone it.

After six weeks of rehabilitation and therapy for both hands, I began to play again. But this time, I vowed to myself never to let this reoccur. I've learned to pace myself to prevent any further damage. I want to keep playing for as long as my hands will allow. It's what I do, and it's all I've ever known. Although there have been times in my life where I've hit rock bottom— whether it be from alcohol, drug abuse, homelessness, or a failed relationship—there has always been one constant I could rely on to lift me from the abyss: my guitar.

27

Here We Go Again

In January of 2011, I flew from Seattle to LA to attend the National Association of Music Merchants, or NAMM. I hadn't been to one of these events since 1992, so I was excited to be going back. It was the same for Randy, Autograph's bassist, as he hadn't attended in years either.

When we met up at the convention, it was like a reunion. We hadn't seen one another since December of 1989, when Autograph split up, twenty-two years prior. We met at the main restaurant of the Anaheim Convention Center and shared a couple of drinks while reminiscing about living on the lunatic fringe all those years ago. During our conversation, we talked about possibly getting together for a reunion tour.

After discussing it for a few minutes, we paused mid-conversation and looked at each other, then both of us said simultaneously, "Naw, ain't gonna happen."

But it did plant a seed . . .

After a bite to eat, Randy and I walked around the convention center to see what new instruments were debuting and to see if we'd run into anyone we knew. We didn't at all expect what happened next. People came at us from everywhere. Old friends, fans, business acquaintances, fellow musicians, merchants, manufacturers—we were surrounded. Pictures were taken, autographs signed. There were lots of hugs, laughing, a few tears, and a lot of smiles. It was all so overwhelming.

Before we entered the convention center, Randy and I thought no one would remember us. Boy, were we wrong. And it felt right. We both knew it. A spark was ignited, and a fire had started within. A reunion was inevitable.

❧

When we parted that evening, the two of us wore big smiles, and our prospective wheels were turning. We realized just how much we missed our old lifestyle of playing live, mingling with the fans, making new friends, creating memories, and just being the court jesters (which we did very well, mind you).

For the time being, a reunion was just a pipe dream. Randy went back to work running his leather shop in LA, and I went back to teaching and managing my music school in Seattle. We touched base a few times but didn't take the idea of playing together again seriously—not at that point, anyway. We both had successful businesses and were pulling in sizable incomes.

Then something completely unexpected happened. Keni Richards, Autograph's original drummer, got in touch with us about doing a reunion. We now had three of the original members showing interest in the idea. But what about our singer, Steve Plunkett? We contacted him, but he gracefully turned it down. He was doing quite well writing music for other artists, movies and tv shows, so he was too busy to take on anything else at that time. He did however give Randy, Keni and I his blessing and said to "Go kick ass and have fun!!"

❧

So, now we have three members that are a go, but we still needed a singer. Keni had a guy in mind who had been referred to him by someone he knew in the industry. (This was while Keni was still alive, obviously.)

After I watched a couple of YouTube videos of the recommended singer, I thought, *Hmmm, this guy might work out well, for the time being anyway.* We all agreed, so we hired him. After all, this was all just to have some fun and make a little extra cash on the side.

Although things seemed to be moving along well, I began to realize there was a gorilla in the room, and the gorilla's name was *meth*. Being fully aware of Keni's usage of heroin and methamphetamine in the past, the main stipulation for me to undertake this new venture was that he be clean, which he promised he would. Unfortunately, this didn't happen. He was still using and wasn't showing up for rehearsal, so, reluctantly, we had to replace him. But we found a replacement rather quickly.

When we first met the drummer, we just sat around talking to get acquainted. Then, we started the audition. After the first song, we thought we may have a contender. After playing the rest of the songs, we thought he'd work fine, so Randy and I decided to hire him as well.

We hit the stage for our first gig mid-January of 2014. The timing was a bit ironic because the original Autograph played their first gig mid-January of 1984, which made it almost exactly thirty years to the date. The show went over very well, and the fans really loved seeing Randy and I on stage together again. It had been twenty-five years since he and I had the pleasure of playing live together and experience the adoration of the fans. Now, we were back in our element and loving every minute of it.

⟨

I discovered that touring in the 2000s was different to touring in the '80s. Bands no longer had the burden of carrying all their equipment with them. Whether it be a club, small hall, casino, festival, or concert arena, the venues now supplied all the speaker systems, lighting, monitors, amplifiers, drums, microphones, and anything else needed for the shows. The band only had to bring guitars and drumsticks, which made things much easier.

Most bands weren't using tour buses either. Instead, everyone flew to events. They no longer had the overhead expense of trucks, buses, drivers, crew, insurance, fuel, extra rooms, per diem, and so on. All these savings meant a larger profit for the artists themselves.

Although I referred to playing these shows as touring, that's not what it was. We only flew out two or three weekends a month to play shows, mostly during the summertime. It was nothing like the back-to-back shows playing auditoriums in the past. In fact, it was a far cry from it. But Randy and I preferred it this way, as we still had our businesses to run during the week.

To save on more on expenses, I personally took on the role of tour manager. After volunteering, I quickly realized it was quite the undertaking. I had to wear many hats, as the position came with a long list of responsibilities. They included being a liaison between booking agents and promoters, managing contracts, arranging transportation, driving, fueling, hotels, backline advance, soundcheck, performance time, set length, meet and greets, hospitality, guest lists, backstage amenities, managing expenses, accounting, event payment, paychecks, taxes, babysitting Randy, babysitting myself, *and* playing in the band.

The last one was the easy part.

Our first year of touring found us all over the map—from LA, California, to Nottingham, England, and everywhere in between. Many of the shows were festivals with numerous bands from the '80s performing, most of which Randy and I knew. We hadn't seen these familiar faces since that era, so for us, it was like a family reunion. To reminisce with all our old buds from the '80s was like revisiting another lifetime. And reconnecting with these legionnaires of rock seemed to put everything back in perspective. We'd all lived and thrived at a unique time in history, never to be repeated. And there we were, doing it all again, full circle.

Another thing that had changed was the groupies. They were older. They had kids, most of whom were grown, and many had grandchildren.

Randy and I prayed none of the kids were ours because we couldn't fathom paying all the back child support. (Ouch!)

I really enjoyed seeing all the old fans, friends, and musicians from the '80s again. Everyone had stories to tell and memories to share. I found it remarkable that Autograph still had so many fans after being absent for two and a half decades. It made me realize just how much of an impact we'd had, and it was far greater than I could have imagined. To have such a positive effect on people is one of the most rewarding experiences ever. And to have the opportunity to do it all again was truly a blessing.

After playing shows for a couple of years, we decided it might be fun to get into the studio to record an extended play (EP) of four to five songs. But I started feeling uninspired while recording the EP. The new material didn't fit the direction I wanted to go musically. For me, the magic just wasn't there.

With the original Autograph members, we all brought a unique perspective to the creation of each song. For example, when we wrote "Turn Up the Radio," we were all in rehearsal together. I got up on stage and started playing what would become the main riff, then Randy got onstage and came up with the next part. Keni then joined in and added the beat, followed by Steve Isham and Steve Plunkett to finish the song. This was not the case when composing the new material. We were all separated so there was no camaraderie in the songwriting process.

We later recorded five new songs to the EP to create a full long play (LP), but again, my heart just wasn't into it. I was happy to just play the original Autograph material and have fun doing so. Fans following an 80s band don't care about new music, they just want to reminisce about the good times with the music they grew to love in their youth'.

After years of playing with the original Autograph and years playing with the other musicians under our banner, I decided it was time for a change. I'd initially planned to play for only a few years, but stayed longer because I loved performing live, reminiscing with old friends, hanging with Randy, mingling with the fans, and making new memories.

The most important component in my decision was that I was beginning to experience carpal tunnel syndrome again, to the point where my hands were cramping so badly it became painful to play on stage. In addition to this, I was starting to get a bit burned out with being the tour manager and general manager, as well as owning and managing a music school in Seattle. Considering all of this, I decided to take a temporary leave from touring. Randy decided to stick with it a little longer, so he was given permission to continue using the Autograph name, so long as *he* remained involved. This was our policy, to always have one original member involved to legally use the name. I wished him happy trails ahead and let him know I'd be back when I saw fit, and when my hands were physically able. Shortly after my decision, Covid hit. Tragically, this not only caused worldwide havoc, but shut down the entertainment industry for the next two years as a result. So, as it turned out, I wouldn't have been playing anyway.

28

Two Lug Nuts, Two Brain Cells, and Two Big Balls

During the time I was running my music school in Seattle, I found myself continuously falling ill. My students were always coming in sick, even though I'd posted a sign in the school entrance that read, *Please do NOT come in if you're sick. We will gladly reschedule your lesson.* Unfortunately, they ignored this. There were times when some were so sick that I wouldn't even allow them into the school, as they could spread the virus to the other students, teachers, and parents.

Even taking this into account, there was one thing that contributed to my illnesses more than anything: Seattle.

My pulmonary specialist discovered I was allergic to some of the molds in the Pacific Northwest. Especially black mold. He informed me that my allergies to the molds, coupled with the cold, damp weather were the main contributors to my illnesses. And to top it off, I'd developed the early stages of Chronic Obstructive Pulmonary Disease (COPD). So, every time I contracted just a common cold, it turned into a severe respiratory infection. The last year I lived in Seattle, I had to rush myself to the hospital emergency room four separate times. The last time, I almost didn't make it.

As I was lying in bed one night, I found my breaths getting shorter, to the point where I began gasping for air. I managed to get out of bed, get dressed, get to my car, and drive to the emergency room. The moment I arrived, I started to pass out, so I leaned against the horn. The emergency room staff ran out and found I was gasping for air, couldn't speak, and was turning blue from lack of oxygen. They immediately wheeled an oxygen tank out to the car as they knew I couldn't be moved. I was almost gone. Once I was able to breathe on my own again, they brought me inside and kept me overnight for observation. That was the fourth time in one year they had to put me on amoxicillin (a powerful antibiotic) and prednisone (a potent steroid) to open my lungs and clear them of infection.

The next morning, when I was released from the hospital, I immediately went to my pulmonary specialist for an evaluation. This is when he gave me the news. He told me I was to leave the Pacific Northwest before winter or else I may not survive. No exceptions.

At this, I thought of all the things I'd have to leave behind. My school, my home, my mom, my brother, my sister, my nieces, my friends, and my hometown. How could I possibly leave? But then I thought, *just yesterday, I almost died, so I don't think I have much of a choice in the matter.*

I asked the doctor where he suggested I move. He recommended either Arizona or Florida. Since I'd grown up in the Pacific Northwest and had lived in Florida previously, I was accustomed to being surrounded by trees and greenery most of my life. In fact, the only time I hadn't lived among lush surroundings were the years I spent in LA from 1978 – 1992. *So, Florida, here I come again!*

It was only two weeks after the doctor's orders that I gave my school away with all its contents to Leon, a good friend and one of the teachers. I rented a 24-foot truck, packed it with all my belongings, attached a trailer with my car in tow, and off I went! To where? I wasn't exactly sure. All I knew was on the morning of July 1, 2016, I was on my way to

Florida. Since I'd already lived in Fort Lauderdale, on the East Coast, I thought I'd try the west side this time. Maybe somewhere near Tampa. Who knows? I was winging it.

One thing I've learned throughout my lifetime is to accept change, take the risk, and go for it. There comes a time to take inventory of who you are and where you wish to be. Before leaving, I bid my farewells to only a few—my mom and brother, my students and staff at the school, and a few friends, (my dad had unfortunately passed at this point). I wanted this to be my personal passage into a new beginning, without sorrowful goodbyes putting weight on my shoulders. This was my life, unbound and with no anchors. I wanted to keep that feeling throughout my travels. I figured I'd inform everyone else of my departure after I reached my destination. That way, there would be no clouds following me on my journey, and the scene in my rear-view mirror would be nothing but clear skies.

❧

Once I was on the road, I realized that I hadn't used the GPS on my new phone yet. So, when I turned it on, to my surprise, the navigation voice had a British accent. Coupled with the truck noise, I couldn't understand a damn thing it was saying. *Oh, Boy,* I thought, *I'm going to be driving aimlessly all the way across the United States.* Not a good way to start out, but I just laughed and shrugged it off. I knew I'd find my way eventually.

For those of you who have never crossed the Great Continental Divide, I must say it's a spectacular sight to behold. It begins in the state of Idaho, crosses over the Rocky Mountains, and comes out onto the plains of Montana. It's absolutely mind-blowing! But it's a lot more fun when traversing it in a smaller vehicle, rather than a 24-foot truck towing a trailer and car. I can assure you, under those conditions, boredom is not an issue.

While traveling up the pass, I ran into road construction. Only one narrow lane was open, bordered by concrete barriers on each side, which made it very difficult to navigate. I kept thinking I was going to hit one of the side barriers and cause the trailer to flip.

Once I reached the summit, I thought, *Whew, I'm in the clear.* But not for long. When I started my descent on the opposite side of the pass, the wind gusts were so severe it felt as though the truck would capsize at any given moment. And to make things even more exciting, there were no guardrails to keep the truck from soaring over the side—a 1,000-foot drop!

As I descended the steep grade, the powerful wind tossed the truck and trailer about violently, making it almost impossible to control. Once I steadied the truck into one lane, the trailer would overcompensate and swerve into the next, which would then force the truck back into that lane. On top of that, the downgrade was so steep that I had to press the brake with all my strength just to slow it down. I was flying down that mountainside as though I were in a NASCAR downhill derby. I watched in horror as the car and trailer went from one side-view mirror to the next—like a drunken sailor leading an inebriated hooker through a hurricane.

When I finally reached the bottom of the pass, I pulled into the first rest area I encountered and found a toilet, which became my throne of thankful prayers for the next half hour.

After that rollercoaster ride from hell, I drove an average of ten hours per day. And I must say, I loved every minute of it. I felt a calm solitude like I'd never experienced before. There was something about traveling 3,200 miles by myself across a continent with everything I own in tow, not knowing where I was going, but having the freedom to embark on such an excursion, that I found truly liberating. New adventure, new home, new life, new me. I highly recommend it to anyone with a free spirit who seeks change. I guarantee you won't regret it. Focus on the positive, put the pedal to the metal, and follow your dream.

On the evening of the fifth day, I reached Atlanta, Georgia, and pulled into a truck stop to fuel up and refresh my coffee for the final leg of the trip. When I came back out, I saw a big trucker standing next to the trailer I was towing. He just looked at me and shook his head.

"What's wrong?" I asked.

He pointed down at one of the trailer wheels. "It only has two lug nuts, and they're rusted. You got lug nuts broken off from the other wheels too, and that the tire pressure is too low," he replied in a thick southern accent.

Now it was my turn to shake my head. "When I rented it, they assured me the trailer had just passed a safety inspection." Obviously, that was not the case.

"Where you driving from?" the old trucker asked.

"Seattle."

"Whoa!" he said, and that southern accent hit the throttle. "Ya' mean ya' drove over da conteenental deevide and all da' way cross 'merica wit two rusted lug nuts holdin' dis whole damn thang tagetter? Boy, yoo got two big balls!"

You may think at this point I wasn't feeling very secure about the remainder of the trip, and you'd be right. But I thought, *What the hell. I've made it this far, I'm gonna go for it.* And that's exactly what I did. I got into the truck cab and drove the remaining eight hours to Tampa with my fingers crossed and butt puckered the whole way.

I reached the city of Clearwater, just west of Tampa, at about 4:00 a.m. I pulled into the first hotel I saw with a lit vacancy sign. Then I peeled my white-knuckled fingers off the steering wheel and *slowly* un-puckered my butt (just to be safe). I got myself a room, carried up my luggage, and literally flopped onto the bed.

I don't think I had many brain cells left at that point. In fact, I believe my cerebral cortex was running on fumes. *Wow! I made it safe and sound,* I thought as I lay there. And then I remembered about what the trucker had said about the two rusted lug nuts and my two big balls. So, I dubbed my journey "Two Lug Nuts, Two Brain Cells, and Two Big Balls."

29

Life Is the Sum of Our Choices

Once I settled into my new place of residence in the beautiful city of Tampa, I noticed something I hadn't experienced for years: I felt great! I was no longer getting sick. I had more energy, was more focused, more creative, more ambitious, and I could breathe! I was amazed at how the change in climate not only improved my health but also made me feel refreshed, giving me new hope along with a whole new perspective. As many can attest, it's difficult to stay positive and keep up your spirits, your drive, determination, creativity, and overall well-being when your health is compromised. But it's something you learn to deal with if need be.

Fortunately, I found I didn't have to suffer from my health issues, that there was an alternative, and that all I needed was a change of scenery. It turned out to be one of the best decisions I'd ever made, and one that probably saved my life.

I loved being back in Florida. Once again, I was experiencing the sun, the white sandy beaches, turquoise water, the warm gulf breeze, palm trees, blue skies, and the laid-back, stress-free lifestyle was an environment I found quite therapeutic. When I went for my first physical checkup, my vitals were better than they'd been in twenty years. My doctor informed me that my blood pressure, heart rate, oxygen level, cholesterol, blood sugar, and so on, were all that of a healthy, middle-aged man. And thankfully, the results have been the same each time I've gone in for my routine checkups.

※

During this transitional period, I delved back into studying the things I love—philosophy, history, sacred geometry, astronomy, science, nature, metaphysics, and a myriad of other topics. I'd become a bit of a data whore (not to be confused with "date-a-whore"). These are things I'd periodically drifted from over the years. But I've learned that straying from your priorities is the consequence of allowing unimportant things to consume your life. As a result, I've learned to recognize when this is occurring and to *not* allow it to persist. I must curtail whatever it is that's causing me to stray and get myself back on track.

The reasons I've studied such a variety of interests over the years is not only for my own personal growth, but to share what I've learned with others and inspire growth along their journey as well. Sharing knowledge is one of the most important gifts one can give. It opens minds and imaginations to numerous perspectives, concepts, and possibilities. Personally, I've always been grateful to the many who've generously shared their knowledge with me over the years. They sparked a fire within me, and that flame has never died out.

For guitar, it's been the same. My desire was not only to learn all the theory possible for my own purpose, but to share what I'd learned with others. And since 1979, I've been teaching in one form or another consistently, right up to this very day.

Through my travels and experiences, I've come to realize that I don't think like most people do. My mental crayon doesn't color within the lines of commonality. All my life, I've considered myself to be an outlier, someone who doesn't quite fit into the shoes of normalcy. In life, there are two paths you can follow: yours, or the one others choose for you.

I've chosen my own. I perceive my path as that of an individual who sits atop a hill gazing upon the village we call humanity. Just observing, from the outside looking in.

I feel the life I live now is for a purpose other than what I'd once thought. And it's one that becomes more defined each day. It is said the two most important events in one's life are the day you are born, and the day you realize why. For me, I was destined to play guitar, write music, evolve, love, travel, experience life, and acknowledge all I've acquired along the way.

At this time in my life, I feel very fortunate to have found that special person who feels the same, one who also wishes to experience all that life has to offer. Her name is Suzanne, and we are basically a reflection of each other. We'd initially met at the beginning of the Van Halen tour back in 1984 when I saw her sitting backstage by herself on top of some equipment cases. She looked so beautiful, yet so out of place at the same time. A classic beauty, not the typical rocker-type you'd expect to meet backstage at a rock concert.

"What are you doing up there?" I asked.

"What are you doing down there?" she replied.

I knew right then there was something special about her. We talked throughout the night and did so again the following night. Over those two nights, we formed a uniquely special bond. Unfortunately, we lost contact because I lived on the West Coast and was always touring, and she lived on the East Coast and was attending college. But, as luck may have it, we reconnected through social media thirty-six years later. And what has transpired since then has been nothing short of miraculous. Now that we're together again, we share all the amazing things life has to offer, and both feel incredibly blessed because of it.

❦

On April 26th, 2022, Randy, my dear friend and musical companion, passed away from a heart attack. This was a profound loss, to say the least. Since starting the band in 1983, I've had to say goodbye to bandmates

Steve Isham and Keni Richards. But losing Randy hit me differently. Not only was his passing tragic, but it made me realize it was the end of the Autograph era.

There's no way to describe the bond that forms when you're a struggling new band making music and traveling from gig to gig together. It transcends time, defies logic, and leaves you exhausted, yet liberated. Somehow, the five of us, misfits as we were, collectively created a unique sound. Even decades later, when I hear "Turn Up the Radio" playing on the airwaves, something undeniably special happens. It's euphoric.

The passing of one of the final founding members may have marked the end of the band, but Autograph's legacy will always live on. I cherish each of these talented brothers and honor what we created and shared with our fans.

I take comfort in knowing that Randy was met at the pearly gates by Steve Isham's big friendly smile, while Keni tosses him a bottle of Jack, yelling "What took you so long, bro?"

We had a tradition before each show of standing in a circle and placing our hands together, then, on the count of three, exclaimed in unison, "Let's Rock!" It became our mantra, our moment to acknowledge the dream we created together, our act of solidarity. Those times are all but a memory now, but a beautiful one at that.

Love ya, my brothers.

❧

After Randy's passing, something unimaginable happened. As you may recall, Randy was given permission to continue performing under the Autograph banner when I took a leave due to carpal tunnel issues, but that privilege didn't apply to anyone who was not an original member. I learned through a social media announcement about their decision to "continue on as Autograph in Randy's name."

HELLO?

There are two founding members, singer Steve Plunkett and myself, who are still here, alive and well. Not to mention original members Keni

Richards and Steve Isham who had previously passed as well.

In response, I had my attorney send them a cease and desist order. They responded by hiring an attorney and sued me, claiming to have rights to the Autograph name. My response to this was to countersue.

An important thing to note is that under common law in the United States, you create trademark rights from the minute you create a mark and a product is sold under that mark. The Autograph marks were established in 1984 and have been in commerce for forty years with radio play, musical recordings (such as three albums with RCA), movies, TV, live performances and video games worldwide. I have always had trademark rights, so it wasn't about getting the name back, it was about being forced to enforce my rights through trademark infringement legal remedies.

Unfortunately, litigation is not a sprint. I had to learn the virtue of patience, as the legal process is an arduous one. Because it operates at such a slow pace, many people get worn down and often feel forced to give in just to avoid the stress, hassles, and cost of litigation. For me, it had the opposite effect: I became more determined to dig in.

We did settle the case, and I'm very pleased with the outcome: I own the name, trademark and logo. Period. I am committed to preserving the Autograph legacy and honoring the original band of brothers.

❧

As a committed educator, instructor and mentor, I have always been actively involved with helping the next generation of musicians develop their craft. Having gone through this experience, I want to help expand their knowledge in learning their legal rights to protect the art they create. I am working with several organizations with the goal of bringing awareness by facilitating resources and aligning efforts to protect those rights.

And, as per the title of this chapter, "Life is the Sum of Our Choices," I made the choice to preserve the legacy of the band I helped to create, and in doing so, Autograph will always be exactly what it was intended to be—a great rock band that wrote some really cool songs and loved their fans like family.

In the fall of 2023, Autograph was invited into the Rock and Roll Hall of Fame Museum. This was quite unexpected, and of course, graciously accepted. On July 24, 2024, we traveled to Cleveland, Ohio to celebrate the unveiling of the exhibit. The signature black guitar with the yellow graph I recorded and toured with in Autograph hangs in the display next to Randy's bass, which he named "Nuns in a Blender."

That's Randy, what can I say?

Regina, Randy's loving wife, was there to donate it in his honor. She was incredibly proud to be there to keep his legacy alive. These guitars, along with the other memorabilia donated, have found their final resting place within those historic walls for all to enjoy.

In my wildest dreams I could never have imagined the overwhelming moment of seeing the exhibit for the first time. It was so surreal. I thought, *How did this happen? Am I really standing here next to my guitar in the Rock and Roll Hall of Fame?*

As I stood in front of the display to give my acceptance speech, I noticed how everyone in attendance listened intently to my every word. Some people were even emotional.

I then asked my girlfriend Suzanne to come up next to me. I got down on my knee, pulled an engagement ring from my pocket, and asked for her hand in marriage. Now everyone was overcome by emotion, including myself, so much so, I'm not even sure she said "Yes" (Just Kidding. Kinda).

I feel incredibly fortunate to represent the legacy of what Autograph created, to honor my Autograph band mate, Steve Plunkett, who is still alive and well, and to honor those who have passed—Randy Rand, Keni Richards, and Steve Isham. It is with them that I share this prestigious honor. It makes all we worked for come full circle.

Thank you, Rock and Roll Hall of Fame, for graciously making this a part of Autograph's legacy. We are eternally grateful.

From the moment I discovered my love for music, I've been driven by passion. From living in a tent to touring with world-renowned rock and roll bands, I lived my truth. Performing, writing music, writing guitar instruction books, and sharing my passion for the guitar with students around the world gave me purpose and created one big, ongoing adventure. I've won awards, traveled, suffered grievous losses, overcome addiction, faced my fears, and always managed to keep going. All these trials and tribulations collectively shaped me into who I am today. I've learned from my successes and failures equally. And even though it's been a rough road at times, I can't imagine things being different. I truly believe we come into this world to learn and evolve through life experiences, both physically and emotionally.

As I age, I reflect on all I've been through and how I got to where I am. And to be quite honest, I wouldn't wish to be a day younger. I find myself to be continually growing, therefore, each year is a new milestone.

My past is full of a variety of unpredictable occurrences, complexities, bizarre events, failures, successes, and a lot of humor, coupled with an abundance of awe and wonderment. So much so that I decided to write this book to share my story. But I still have many chapters to write, for many more adventures lie ahead.

30

In Closing

Thinking back, I feel there is a part of me that is, and always will be, that fifteen-year-old kid living in a tent in the middle of a blackberry field with a Coleman heater, lamp, amplifier, a guitar, and a dream. Many things have changed since then, but in my heart, not much has. When I look back from then to now, I think about what an incredible adventure it's all been . . . and I wouldn't change a thing.

Until next time . . .

Love and peace to you all.

THE END

Acknowledgments

A very special thanks to Suzanne. You are the guiding light that shines on the path we walk together. I love you with all my heart.

To my family, my parents- Victor and Harriett, my sisters Mari, Cheryl, Cindy and Sheila, and my brother, John, for their love, encouragement, and continued support. And to my nieces and nephews, Erica, Nicole, Ryan, Kami, Maggie, Christina, Angela, and Michael. You mean the world to me, and I love you all! And last but not least, Alex, who is like a loving daughter to me.

A special thanks to Warren Bleeker and Eric Kohli of the law firm Lewis-Roca for helping to preserve the Autograph legacy. You guys are the best!

And to all my friends, who have always been there for me. .. and still are. Thank you!

And to the people who inspired me along my journey while writing this book:
Randy Rand
Regina Rand
Steve Plunkett

Keni Richards
Steve Isham
Jeff West
Dan Gray
Chuck and Ruby Simmons
Mark Stanley
Jay Blumenstock
Rob Ricketts
Jay Likeness
Leslie Rule
Lisa Manale
Mike Santagata
Rachel Cone-Gorham

Photography:
Joe Schaeffer
Michael Cox
Greg Thomas
Tim McMahon
Glen LaFerman
Mark Weiss
Neil Zlozower
Traci Roher
Cortney Bury
Bill Bungard
Chris DeFrancesco
David Plastik
Dawn Osborne
Mark Rockinon

Images

Uhhh . . . I really don't know what to say about this. Lol! My mom told me, years later when she showed me this picture, that my dad fell asleep when he was supposed to show me how to eat corn on the cob. We both laughed hysterically!

This is a picture of me and my older sisters Mari (left) and Cheryl (right) dressed up for Easter Mass. Notice they are not holding my hands, they're holding my shirt sleeves so I won't run away and hide. I wasn't particularly fond of church, even at that age.

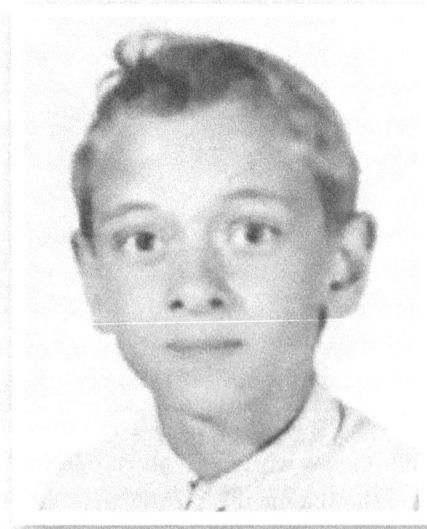

This is a picture of me at age eight. Don't let the innocent look fool you, as I was anything but!

Here is a letter to my parents from the school board about my behavior and truancy. I only went to fifty-one days of school that year. I liked school about as much as I liked church.

From 1973, this was one of the first bands I played in.. Previously, there was Outlawd', and then there was this one called The Ross Taylor Band, even though there was no Ross Taylor. We thought it would be clever to have a fictitious name like Jethro Tull, but we found out later that Jethro Tull was an actual character who was an 18th-century agriculturist. The joke was on us!

Here is a picture of me with my black and white Fender Stratocaster in 1975.

Here is a shot of me playing live with that same guitar, circa 1975.

This is a band I was in from 1976-1977 called Silverlode. It was the last band I played in from the Seattle area before moving to Los Angeles in late 1977.

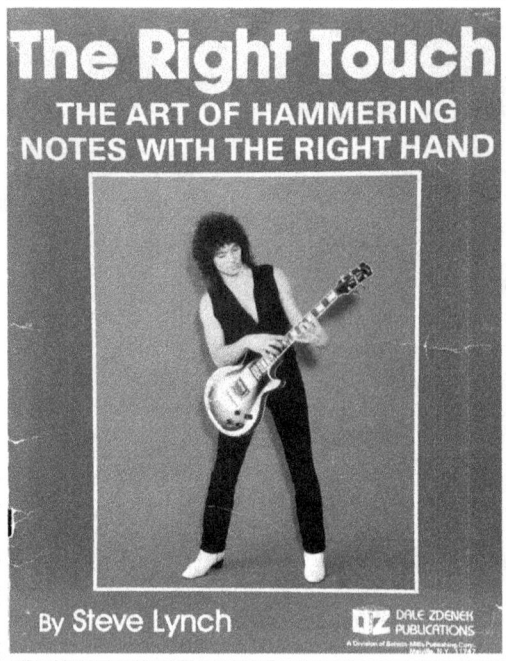

Here is the first book I wrote about the two-handed hammer-on or tapping technique called *The Right Touch*. I wrote it while attending the Guitar Institute of Technology in Hollywood in 1978-1979.

At the Record Plant in LA recording Autograph's first RCA album *Sign in Please* in 1984.

Another picture while recording at the Record Plant, with myself in the foreground recording some solos and our drummer Keni in the background looking a bit bewildered . . . which was usually the case.

Backstage passes while touring with Van Halen in 1984. The one on the left is for Madison Square Garden, which is where we signed our initial deal with RCA Records.

In 1984, I won the Guitarist of the Year Award for the New York Music Expo. Notice the petrified look on my face. That's because I was sitting on the stage at Madison Square Garden with (L-R) Al Di Meola, Les Paul, Johnny Winter, myself, and jazz great Larry Coryell. I had to get up and play for five minutes by myself . . . in front of them, which, to my surprise, they loved!

One of Autograph's early promo photos . We were on our way!

A shot of me playing live while Autograph toured with Mötley Crüe in 1986.

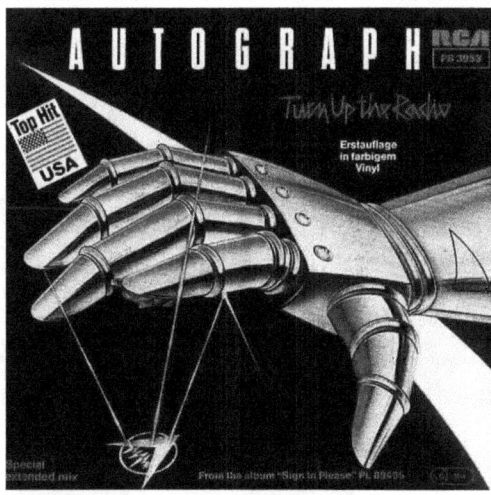

The cover for our first RCA album *Sign in Please* from 1984.

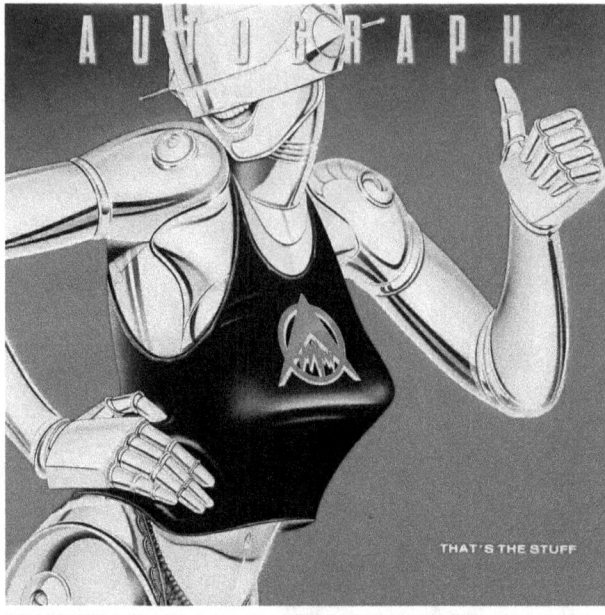

The cover of our second RCA album, *That's the Stuff*, from 1985.

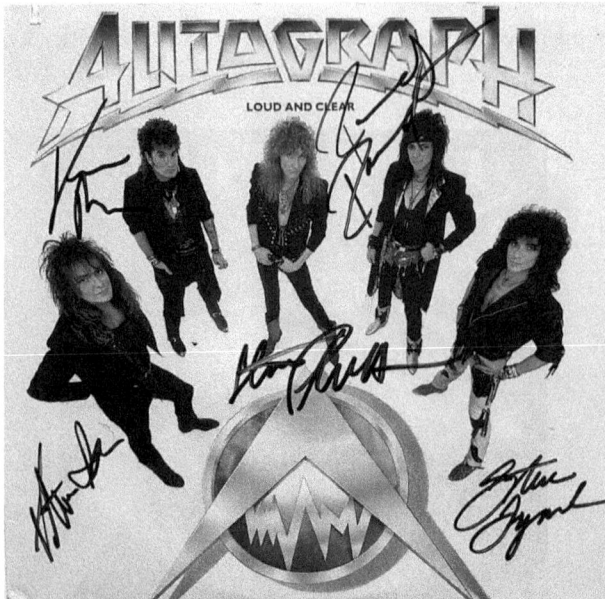

The cover of our third RCA album, *Loud and Clear*, from 1987.

From 1979, a throwback picture with my 1955 Les Paul Custom.

From 1987, this is from a photoshoot at Lion Share Recording Studio for Crate amplifiers.

Steve Lynch & CRATE

Another promo photo for Crate from 1987.

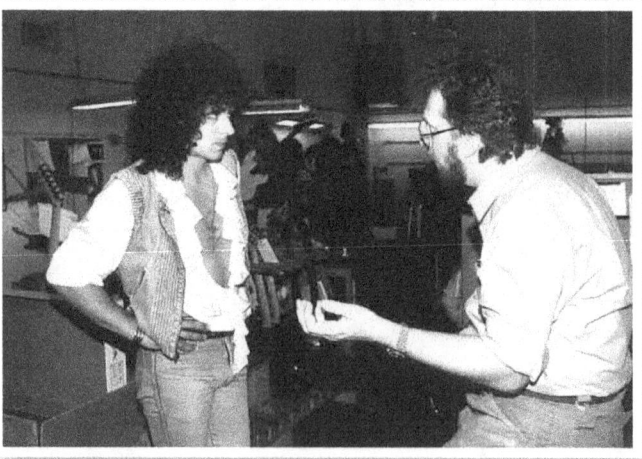

Talking with Grover Jackson from Jackson Guitars at the factory in San Dimas in 1985. This is when we designed my signature model guitar.

A throwback photo I found from Mike Varney's "Spotlight" column in *Guitar Player* magazine from January 1983. It was the first column he'd written for them and the first time I'd been featured in a guitar magazine.

A picture from the video shoot for the song "Loud and Clear." We invited Vince Neil from Mötley Crüe and Ozzy Osborne to make an appearance, which they gladly agreed to since we were all good friends.

00 GREATEST GUITAR SOLOS

Autograph: guitarist Steve Lynch, second from the right.

49 *Turn Up The Radio*
STEVE LYNCH
From: *Autograph - Sign In Please, 1984*

The mind boggles as to how Pasadena glam-rockers Autograph   The solo in *Turn Up The Radio* is the perfect demonstration of this.

This is from an article about the best guitar solos of all time. I was voted in at number 49 for the solo in "Turn Up the Radio," just one before Jimi Hendrix, who was number 50. Who could have seen that coming? Lol!

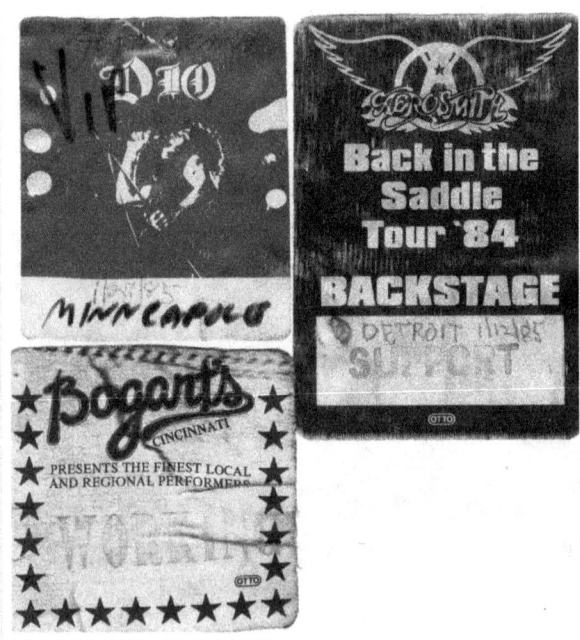

Backstage passes while on tour with Dio and Aerosmith, 1985.

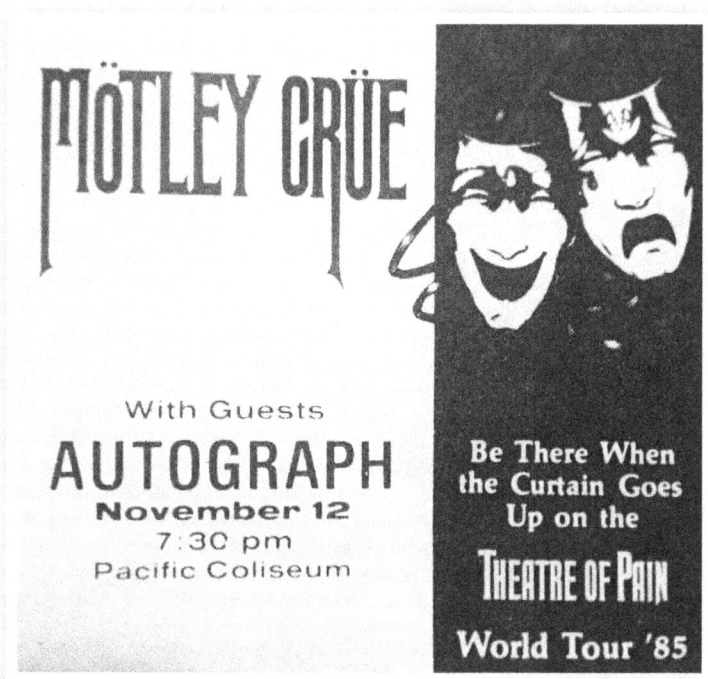

Promo patch and backstage pass while touring with Mötley, 1986.

Flashback pic of Savoy Brown from 1980-1981. From L-R: Keith Boyce, Kim Simmons, Tim Bogert, Ralph Mormon, and myself.

We were in most of the popular '80s rock magazines, but this one from *Hit Parader* was one of my favorites.

One of those "poser" shots from a guitar mag . . . I always hated posing for these. Lol!

Our first time on *American Bandstand* with the one-and-only Dick Clark! We were beyond excited about this epic episode in our lives! Dick and his wife were the most gracious people you could ever meet, and the two of them ran the whole show. Wow! They even invited us back!

Talking one-on-one with the man himself. And look! We're the same height! Now that's "big" time. Haha!

Photo from the filming of the "Dance All Night" video from our *Loud and Clear* album in 1987. Really had a blast on this!

This is a shot that photographer Glen La Ferman took as a promo for Jackson Guitars in 1985. The power went out during the shoot because it took a bank of lights to get us all lit . . . not in the way you're thinking. It was for brightness. Jeez!

This is a promo shot from 1985… lookin' slim and trim.

A live picture from the video shoot for *Loud and Clear*.

STEVE
LYNCH

Musical Profile by Wolf Marshall

When this picture was taken for another guitar magazine, it was after we'd just toured with Aerosmith, Brian Adams, Dio, and Heart. As you can see by the vagueness in my eyes, I was a bit burned out . . . as in *no one was home*.

I must have drunk something that tasted nasty . . . lol. This is a pic from an outdoor festival in Texas in 1988.

A picture is worth a thousand words. At least this one is. It's when we received our Gold Albums! Yeah, we were in LaLa Land . . . in a very good way!

USA Gold Album, 1985.

Canadian Gold Album, 1985.

(c) dirk.ballerstaedt

My "show-off" wall, 1987

Promo shot for Westone Guitars in 1988. Loved my personalized license plate . . . lol! I eventually had to trade it out for a regular one, there were just too many looky-loos.

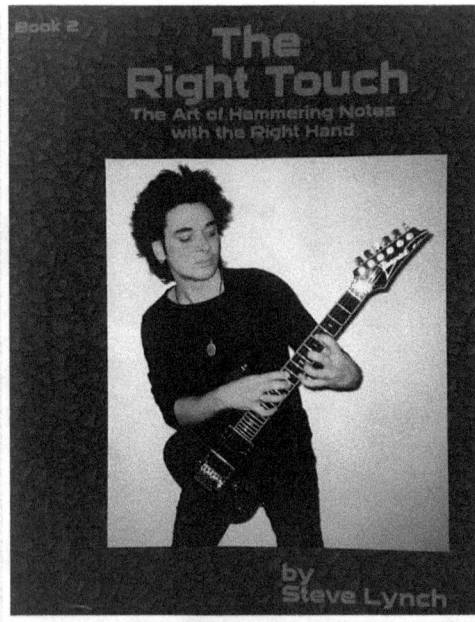

The second *Right Touch* instructional book was written in 1987 and rereleased in 2004. My third *Right Touch* book was written in 1988 and was also rereleased in 2004. They were both quite a bit more advanced than the first one from 1979.

Here is the cover shot for my REH instructional video *The Two-Handed Guitarist* filmed in 1987. My old teacher from Seattle was the director . . . and that scared the hell out of me! Lol

Cruisin' LA in the Benz . . . life is good! I remember thinking, *I wish I were me.*

My solo album, *Network 23*, which I think is by far some of my best work. I played all the instruments except drums and vocals. I also wrote all the music and a good share of the lyrics and produced it myself. It was recorded in 1992-1994.

My favorite place in the world . . . the forest. This was taken when I moved back up to Seattle in the late 1990s. I used to hike the hundreds of trails all over the Pacific Northwest and was never disappointed with the breathtaking views and the solitude I found there.

This is from a photo shoot we did in Montana with photographer Cortney Bury, circa 2016.

A photo from when I was filming my instructional site *lynchlicks.com*. We videoed 100 guitar licks and 18 guitar solos with a breakdown of how to play them, and we did it over one weekend. Believe me . . . my hands hated me.

The benefit for Kids with Cancer was the most fulfilling fundraiser I'd ever been involved with. My special thanks go out to Joe Black and all those who made this very important event possible.

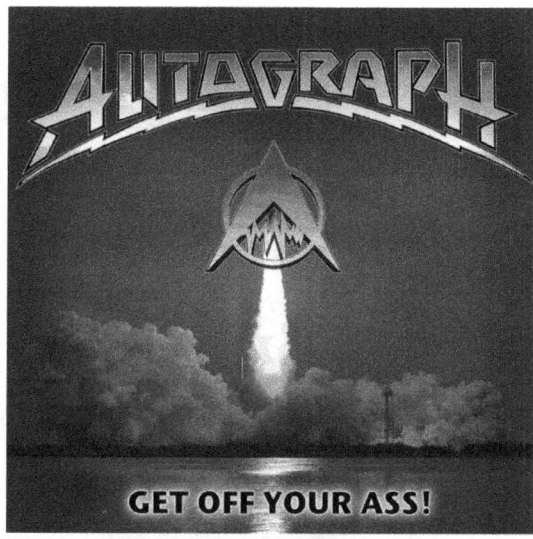

This is the cover for an album Randy Rand and I did in 2017 with a couple of musicians who were not part of the original Autograph lineup. Unfortunately, I was dissatisfied with the outcome. Without the original lineup writing and recording together like in the old days, I felt it fell short of what used to be.

Here is a live shot from the Monsters of Rock Cruise in 2018 after I completed my guitar solo in front of a packed audience. This reaction was not intended. It's just the way the audience's roar made me feel— absolutely elated!

A live shot from the M3 Festival in Columbia, Maryland, in 2015. A large portion of my family (including sisters, nieces, nephews, great-nieces, and great-nephews came out to see me play, some for the first time. I couldn't have enjoyed this day more.

Warming up at soundcheck, thinking about the gig that night. What a wonderful feeling.

Playing a Dean guitar version of my Jackson from the '80s, black with a yellow graph. I designed it to have that graph on it to reflect the name of the band: *Auto-graph*.

Live shot of me playing my solo at Firefest in Nottingham, England.

Randy and I doing what we did best on stage—goofing around and smiling a lot . . . just having fun.

This is a picture from a photographer at Firefest in England. I absolutely loved playing to these crowds! And the audience let us know they loved it as well. There was thunderous applause after each song.

Another venue . . . another promo shot . . . this never gets old. I love every minute of it.

Backstage checking my gear before showtime. This is right before the fun begins!

Lazie Indie Magazine

Edition 11
March 2021

Dr. Jassie Gift
Briana Dinsdale
Richard Lynch

Andrew Featherstone
Elektrohorse
Randy Skaggs

Stanley
Ej Oullette

Canal Radio
Carl & The Reda Mafia

Cover Story
Steve Lynch

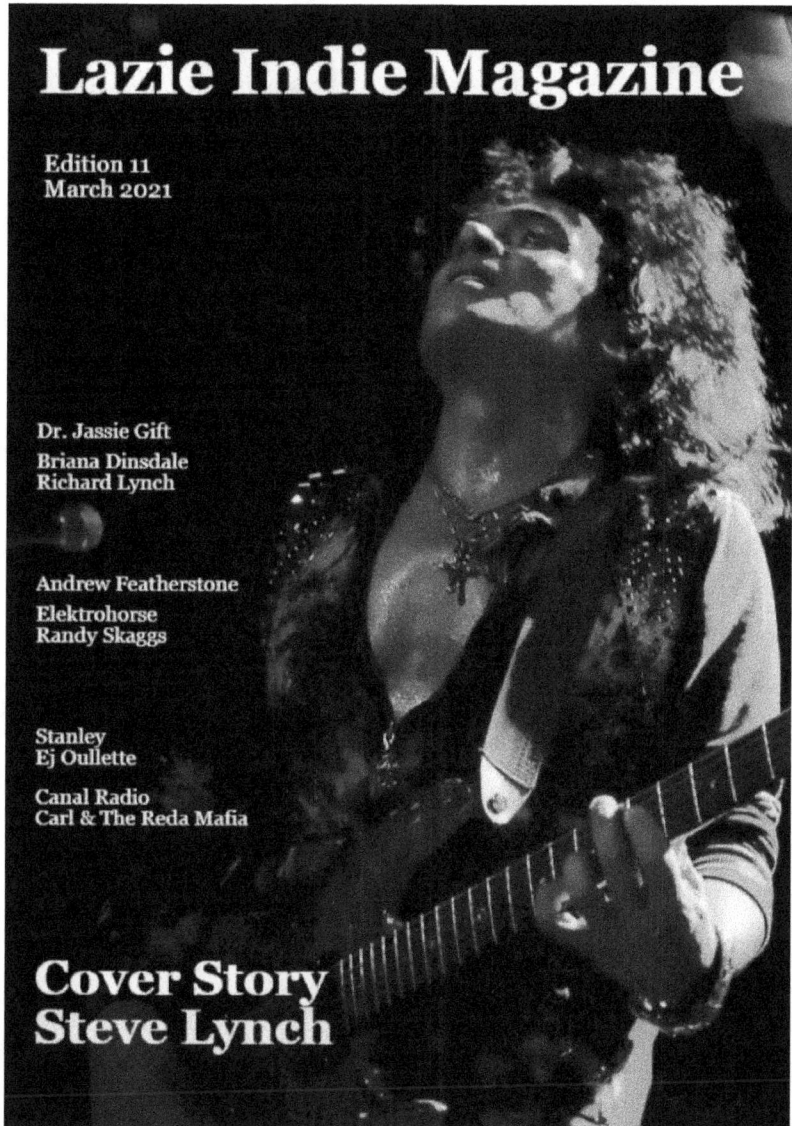

This is the cover of *Lazie Indie Magazine*, which is an international magazine based out of India. They did an amazing interview with me.

I'd never in my life grown my beard out before this, so it took a while to get used to it.

My sweet love Suzanne and I enjoying our lives in Florida. The girl of my dreams. Now we're living our dreams together.

At the Rock & Roll Hall of Fame when Suzanne and I got engaged. I thought it was the perfect time to pop the question... and she said yes!!

The unveiling of my signature Autograph black guitar with the yellow graph at the Rock & Roll Hall of Fame. Randy's bass (Nuns in a Blender) is just below it, along with other Autograph memorabilia.

About the Author

S teve Lynch started playing bass guitar in 1968 but switched over to guitar the day Jimi Hendrix died: September 18th, 1970. He played in various Seattle based bands from 1973-1978, including Yellow Dog, Outlawed, The Ross Taylor Band, and Silverload.

In 1978 Steve enrolled and was accepted into The Guitar Institute of Technology. He graduated in 1979 earning the Guitarist of The Year and Most Likely to Succeed awards, along with various other extra curriculum merits. While attending The Guitar Institute, Steve wrote his first book *The Right Touch*, a book about playing notes on the fingerboard of the guitar with four fingers on each hand. The book was published immediately by Zdenek Publications and was later picked up by Belwyn Mills and soon after by Warner Brothers Publications. The book was a best seller in its category worldwide.

After Steve Graduated from GIT and published his first book, he went on to do session work in the LA recording mecca, recording with various artists from Warner Brothers and Greg Lake from Emerson, Lake and Palmer fame. He then started playing the live local scene with a variety of bands until 1983, when he co-formed RCA recording artist,

Autograph. In this project he toured with the likes of Van Halen, Mötley Crüe, Aerosmith, Ronnie James Dio, Whitesnake, Brian Adams, Heart, and so on. They had the hit "Turn Up the Radio" as well as various other radio-friendly songs that helped earn them the reputation as being a top contender in the '80s rock scene. The band eventually sold over five million albums worldwide out of the three that were recorded for RCA.

During the time with Autograph Steve wrote columns on his technique and interviews for *Guitar Player, Guitar World,* and *Guitar for the Practicing Musician* as well as various international music magazines. Steve won the Solo of the Year Award for "Turn Up the Radio" in 1985. He also won Guitarist of the Year Award at the New York Guitar Expo in 1985. He also published two more books (*The Right Touch Books* 2 and 3) and an instructional video titled The Two-Handed Guitarist about his two-handed technique and lead guitar work with Autograph. This, along with the recognition of his work with Autograph made him a well known and respected name in the international guitar community. After Autograph, Steve taught 325 clinics in twenty countries promoting his books and instructional videos.

In 1994-95 Steve recorded his first solo album titled Network 23, where he showed a more extensive view of his guitar techniques as well as songwriting, arranging, and producing. He wrote all the music and played all guitar parts including bass, keyboards, background vocals, percussion, and drum sampling. Autograph soon after released an album of demos previously unreleased on an album called Missing Pieces.

In 1996 Steve relocated back to Seattle and opened up his own music school called The Federal Way School of Music. He ran the school for twenty years then moved to Palm Harbor Florida in 2016 where he now resides. In 2013 Steve and Randy Rand, the original bassist, decided to reform Autograph (with the exception of a new hired singer and drummer). They released an album, "Get Off Your Ass," and toured again for several years in the US and abroad.

In 2024 Autograph was welcomed into the Rock and Roll Hall of Fame in Cleveland, Ohio, Steve donated his legendary guitar and one of Randy's basses as well as Autograph memorabilia from the eighties for display in the museum.

www.ingramcontent.com/pod-product-compliance
Lightning Source LLC
Chambersburg PA
CBHW070344090426
42733CB00009B/1278